MASTERING
WEALTH

MASTERING WEALTH

THE STOCK MARKET GITA FOR FINANCIAL FREEDOM

DR ASHISH VAJPAYEE

Contents

Acknowledgement————————————————————————3
Overview————————————————————————————4
I. Introduction————————————————————————————7
  A. Overview of the Bhagavad Gita
  B. Importance of wealth in human life
II. Understanding Wealth——————————————————————13
  A. Definition of wealth according to the Bhagavad Gita
  B. Different types of wealth (material, spiritual, emotional)
  C. Importance of balance and moderation in wealth accumulation
III. Principles of Wealth Mastery————————————————21
  A. Karma Yoga - Performing actions selflessly and diligently
  B. Dharma - Following one's duty and responsibilities
  C. Detachment - Not being attached to the fruits of actions
  D. Generosity - Sharing wealth with others
  E. Discipline - Managing wealth with discipline and integrity
  F. Knowledge - Acquiring financial literacy and understanding wealth management
IV. Wealth and Happiness——————————————————————38
  A. Relationship between wealth and happiness
  B. Importance of inner fulfillment and contentment
  C. Balancing material prosperity with spiritual well-being
V. Challenges and Obstacles————————————————————42
  A. Greed and attachment to wealth
  B. Overcoming the fear of loss
  C. Dealing with financial difficulties and setbacks
VI. Practical Strategies——————————————————————45
  A. Taking the First Steps: A Beginner's Guide to Entering the Market
  B. Budgeting and financial planning
  C. Investing wisely and ethically

D. Giving back to society through charity and service
E. Seeking guidance from mentors and experts
VII. Conclusion--177
A. Recap of key teachings from the Bhagavad Gita on wealth mastery
B. Importance of applying spiritual principles in financial matters
C. Achieving holistic prosperity and well-being through balanced wealth management

Acknowledgement

"To my beloved parents, whose love, support, and guidance have been the foundation of my journey to understanding wealth and freedom, to the divine presence of God, whose blessings and grace illuminate every step of this path toward financial abundance and fulfilment And to the timeless wisdom of the Bhagavad Gita, which illuminates the path to self-realization and prosperity."

This book is dedicated to you, with gratitude and reverence.

Overview

Thank you for taking the time to read my book. Hello, this is Dr Ashish Vajpayee (09/09/2023) Welcoming you to "Mastering Wealth : The Stock Market Gita for Financial Freedom" a transformative guide to navigating the complex landscape of wealth with wisdom, purpose, and abundance. In this book, we explore the profound teachings of the Bhagavad Gita to unlock the secrets of true wealth—material, spiritual, and emotional.

Key Themes:

The Multifaceted Nature of Wealth: Discover the deeper dimensions of wealth beyond mere material possessions.

Karma Yoga and Selfless Action: Learn how selfless action leads to abundance and fulfillment.

Happiness and Wealth: Explore the relationship between wealth and true happiness.

Wise Investing and Financial Planning: Master the art of financial management with expertise and ethics.

Charity and Service: Enrich your life and the lives of others through the power of giving.

Chapter Breakdown:
The Essence of Wealth: Understanding the true meaning and purpose of wealth.

Karma Yoga: The Path to Abundance: Embracing selfless action as the key to wealth and fulfillment.

Wealth and Happiness: Finding joy and contentment in wealth beyond materialism.

Investing with Wisdom: Ethical and sustainable strategies for building wealth.

Financial Planning for Prosperity: Practical tools for budgeting, saving, and investing.

Enriching Lives Through Charity: The transformative power of generosity and service.

Unique Approach:

"Mastering Wealth" blends ancient wisdom with modern insights, offering a holistic approach to wealth mastery. Through a combination of practical strategies, spiritual principles, and real-life examples, this book equips you with the knowledge and tools to thrive in your financial journey.

Benefits for Readers:
By reading "Mastering Wealth," you will:

Gain a deeper understanding of wealth and its various dimensions.

Learn practical strategies for financial management and investing.
Discover the joy of giving back and making a positive impact.
Find greater happiness and fulfillment in your wealth journey.

Conclusion:

Embark on a journey of transformation and empowerment with "Mastering Wealth." Whether you're a seasoned investor, a budding entrepreneur, or someone seeking a more meaningful relationship with wealth, this book is your guide to unlocking abundance and prosperity in every aspect of life.

Introduction

As we know Bhagavad-gita is divided in three parts as:
Chapter 1-6   Karma yoga
Chapter 7-12   Bhakti yoga
Chapter 13-18 Jnana yoga

Same I have attempted to divide chapters of this book "Mastering Wealth: The Stock Market Gita for Financial Freedom" in three parts as:
Chapter 1-4   Karma yoga(Actions)
Chapter 5-6   Bhakti yoga(Discipline)
Chapter 7   Jnana yoga(Knowledge)

A. Unlocking the Wisdom of the Bhagavad Gita

Once upon a time in a busy city, there lived a young entrepreneur named Darshan Patel. Despite his business acumen and hard work, Darshan often found himself feeling overwhelmed by the pressures of wealth and success. He yearned for a deeper understanding of how to navigate the complexities of wealth while staying true to his values.

One day, Darshan came across an old bookstore tucked away in a quiet corner of the city. Intrigued, he stepped inside and found himself drawn to a dusty old bookshelf.

Among the books, one title caught his eye: "Mastering Wealth: The Stock Market Gita for Financial Freedom"

Curious, Darshan picked up the book and began reading. As he delved into the ancient teachings of the Bhagavad Gita, he was struck by the timeless wisdom it offered on the subject of wealth mastery. The Gita spoke of balancing material success with spiritual fulfillment, of performing actions selflessly, and of the importance of discipline and integrity in managing wealth.

Darshan found himself captivated by the stories and lessons within the Gita. He learned about Karma Yoga and the power of selfless action, about Dharma and the importance of aligning wealth with one's duty and responsibilities. He discovered the concept of detachment, freeing himself from the chains of attachment to wealth, and embracing generosity as a way to create abundance for others as well as himself.

As Darshan immersed himself deeper into the teachings, he began to apply them in his business and personal life. He started practicing mindfulness and gratitude, finding joy not just in financial success but also in the simple moments of life. He became more disciplined in his financial management, making wise investment choices and giving back to the community through charitable endeavors.

Over time, Darshan noticed a profound transformation within himself. He felt a sense of inner peace and contentment that transcended mere material wealth. He realized that true mastery of wealth wasn't just about accumulating riches but about living a balanced and fulfilling life in harmony with oneself and others.

Armed with the wisdom of the Bhagavad Gita, Darshan became not just a successful entrepreneur but also a beacon of inspiration for others seeking to master wealth with integrity and wisdom. He shared his journey and the teachings of the Gita with fellow entrepreneurs, guiding them on a path of holistic prosperity and well-being.
And so, the story of Darshan and the Bhagavad Gita's timeless wisdom spread far and wide, touching the lives of many who sought to unlock the secrets of mastering wealth in today's ever-changingworld.

B. The Significance of Wealth in Human Life

The significance of wealth in human life encompasses various aspects that contribute to individual well-being and societal progress:

(A) Basic Needs Fulfillment: Wealth plays a crucial role in meeting basic human needs such as food, shelter, clothing, and healthcare. It ensures a standard of living that supports physical health and overall quality of life.

(B)-Opportunity Creation: Wealth creates opportunities for personal and professional growth. It enables access to education, skill development, career advancement, and entrepreneurship, empowering individuals to achieve their full potential.

(C)-Security and Stability: Financial wealth provides security and stability, offering a safety net against unforeseen circumstances such as emergencies, health issues, or economic downturns. It fosters resilience and confidence in navigating life's challenges.

(D)-Quality of Life Enhancement: Wealth enhances the quality of life by enabling access to amenities, leisure activities, travel, cultural experiences, and entertainment. It contributes to comfort, convenience, and enjoyment in daily living.

(E)-Empowerment and Autonomy: Wealth empowers individuals to make autonomous decisions and choices aligned with their values, preferences, and aspirations. It fosters a sense of independence, freedom, and self-determination.

(F)-Contribution to Society: Wealth can be leveraged for positive impact and contribution to society. Through philanthropy, charitable giving, social investments, and community initiatives, individuals can address social issues, support vulnerable populations, and drive positive change.

(G)-Generational Legacy: Wealth management allows for the creation of a lasting legacy that benefits future generations. It enables the transfer of assets, values, knowledge, and opportunities, ensuring continuity and prosperity across generations.

(H)-Economic Growth and Development: Individual wealth accumulation contributes to overall economic growth and development. It stimulates investment, innovation, job creation, infrastructure development, and economic prosperity, benefiting society as a whole.

While acknowledging the significance of wealth, it's essential to emphasize the importance of responsible wealth management, ethical practices, equitable distribution, and social responsibility. A holistic approach to wealth considers not only financial prosperity but also emotional well-being, environmental sustainability, social justice, and ethical leadership, fostering a more inclusive and equitable society.

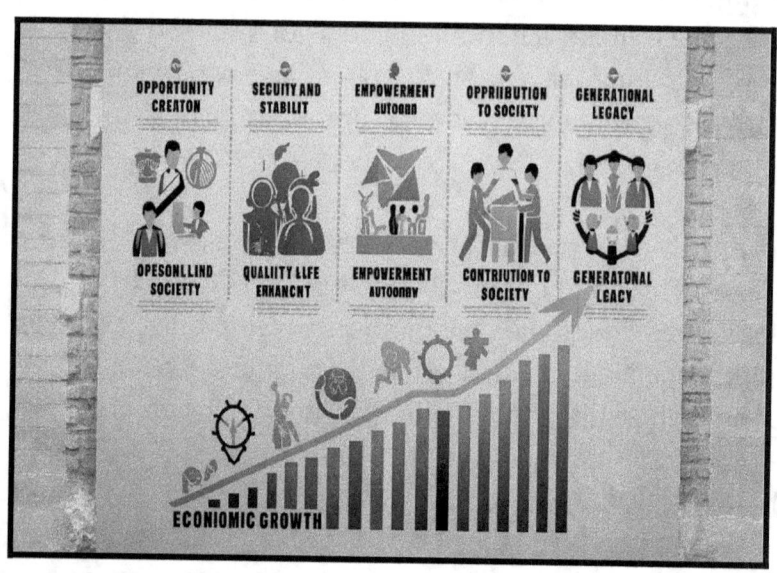

II. Understanding Wealth
A. Definition of wealth according to the Bhagavad Gita

In the Bhagavad Gita, wealth is not limited to material possessions or financial assets. Instead, wealth is viewed in a broader and more holistic sense, encompassing various aspects of life. Here's a definition of wealth according to the Bhagavad Gita:

Wealth, according to the Bhagavad Gita, is the abundance of virtues, knowledge, inner peace, contentment, compassion, and spiritual wisdom that leads to holistic well-being and fulfillment. It includes material prosperity but extends beyond mere possessions to encompass the richness of one's character, relationships, values, and connection with the divine. True wealth is measured not just by external riches but by inner virtues and spiritual growth, ultimately leading to a life of purpose, harmony, and transcendence.

A(a). Defining True Wealth: Insights from the Gita

True wealth, as elucidated in the Bhagavad Gita, transcends mere material possessions. It encompasses a profound abundance of virtues, wisdom, and inner fulfillment that leads to holistic well-being.

Here are key insights from the Gita on defining true wealth:

1-Virtues Over Riches: The Gita emphasizes the importance of cultivating virtues such as integrity, compassion, humility, and courage as the true markers of wealth. These inner qualities bring lasting fulfillment and contribute to a meaningful life.

2-Knowledge and Wisdom: True wealth includes the acquisition of knowledge and spiritual wisdom. It involves self-awareness, self-realization, and a deep understanding of the interconnectedness of all beings and the universe.

3-Inner Peace and Contentment: Wealth, according to the Gita, is also measured by inner peace and contentment. It arises from detachment, acceptance of the present moment, and alignment with one's higher purpose.

4-Service and Generosity: The Gita teaches that true wealth is not hoarded but shared selflessly with others. Acts of kindness generosity, and service to humanity are regarded as invaluable forms of wealth.

5-Spiritual Growth: Wealth is seen as a means for spiritual growth and self-transcendence. It involves the cultivation of devotion, gratitude, and a deep connection with the divine, leading to inner transformation and enlightenment.

6-Balance and Harmony: True wealth encompasses a balance between material prosperity and spiritual well-being. It involves harmonizing worldly responsibilities with spiritual practices, leading to a harmonious and fulfilling life.

7-Legacy of Goodness: Building a legacy of goodness and positive impact is considered true wealth. Leaving behind a legacy of love,
compassion, and positive influence on others is valued more than material inheritance.

In essence, the Bhagavad Gita's insights on true wealth emphasize the holistic nature of prosperity, encompassing inner virtues, spiritual growth, service to others, and a balanced approach to life. It invites individuals to redefine their understanding of wealth and pursue a path of meaningful abundance that enriches not only oneself but also the world around them.

B. The Multifaceted Nature of Wealth: Material, Spiritual, Emotional

Material Wealth

Material wealth refers to the tangible and measurable assets that contribute to an individual's financial prosperity and well-being. It encompasses various aspects such as:

1-Financial Assets: These include money in bank accounts, investments in stocks, bonds, mutual funds, and other financial instruments that generate income or appreciate in value over time.

2-Real Estate: Property ownership, including residential homes, commercial buildings, land, and other real estate assets, adds to one's material wealth.

3-Possessions: Material possessions such as vehicles, jewelry, electronic gadgets, artwork, and other valuable items also contribute to one's wealth.

4-Income: A steady and substantial income from employment, business ventures, investments, or other sources is crucial for building and maintaining material wealth.

5-Standard of Living: Material wealth often translates into a higher standard of living, affording access to better housing, healthcare, education, travel, leisure activities, and luxuries.

While material wealth is important for financial stability, comfort, and achieving certain life goals, it's essential to recognize that true wealth encompasses more than just material possessions. Balancing material wealth with spiritual fulfillment, emotional well-being, and meaningful relationships is key to leading a truly rich and fulfilling life.

Spiritual Wealth

Spiritual wealth refers to the inner abundance, fulfillment, and sense of purpose that comes from connecting with one's spiritual essence, values, and beliefs. It encompasses several key aspects:

1-Inner Peace and Harmony: Spiritual wealth is often associated with a deep sense of inner peace, tranquility, and harmony. This inner calmness arises from practices such as meditation, mindfulness, prayer, and contemplation, which help individuals align with their spiritual nature and find solace amidst life's challenges.

2-Purpose and Meaning: Spiritual wealth involves understanding one's purpose in life and living in alignment with one's core values, beliefs, and aspirations. It's about finding meaning and fulfillment in everyday experiences and activities, and contributing positively to the world around us.

3-Connection to Something Greater: Many people derive spiritual wealth from their connection to a higher power, universal consciousness, or the divine. This connection provides a sense of guidance, support, and belonging, fostering feelings of awe, reverence, and gratitude for the mysteries of existence.

4-Compassion and Empathy: Spiritual wealth often leads to increased compassion, empathy, and kindness towards oneself and others. It involves cultivating qualities such as forgiveness, generosity, acceptance, and unconditional love, which enhance relationships and contribute to a more harmonious and compassionate society.

5-Wisdom and Insight: Spiritual wealth includes the development of wisdom, insight, and inner knowing that transcend mere intellectual knowledge. It involves accessing intuitive guidance, discerning deeper truths, and experiencing moments of clarity and enlightenment that enrich one's life journey.

Ultimately, spiritual wealth is not dependent on external circumstances or material possessions but is nurtured through self-awareness, personal growth, and a deepening connection to the spiritual dimensions of life. It plays a vital role in holistic well-being and contributes significantly to a fulfilling and meaningful existence.

Emotional Wealth

Emotional wealth refers to the richness and well-being experienced in one's emotional life. It encompasses various dimensions that contribute to overall emotional health and fulfillment:

1-Emotional Resilience: Emotional wealth involves developing resilience to navigate life's challenges, setbacks, and uncertainties. It includes the ability to bounce back from adversity, cope with stress effectively, and maintain a positive outlook even during difficult times.

2-Self-Awareness and Emotional Intelligence: Emotional wealth is enhanced through self-awareness, which involves understanding one's emotions, thoughts, and behaviors. Emotional intelligence, including skills like empathy, self-regulation, social awareness, and interpersonal communication, plays a crucial role in building healthy relationships and managing emotions effectively.

3-Positive Relationships: Emotional wealth is fostered through meaningful and supportive relationships with family, friends, colleagues, and community members. Strong social connections, trust, mutual respect, and open communication contribute to emotional well-being and a sense of belonging.

4-Gratitude and Positive Emotions: Cultivating gratitude, appreciation, and a focus on positive emotions like joy, love, compassion, and contentment enhances emotional wealth. Practicing mindfulness, gratitude journaling, acts of kindness, and savoring positive experiences can uplift mood and overall well-being.

5-Self-Care and Well-Being Practices: Prioritizing self-care, including physical, mental, and emotional health practices such as exercise, adequate sleep, healthy nutrition, relaxation techniques, and seeking professional support when needed, contributes to emotional wealth and overall life satisfaction.

6-Purpose and Meaningful Goals: Having a sense of purpose, pursuing meaningful goals aligned with personal values, and engaging in activities that bring fulfillment and satisfaction contribute to emotional wealth. Feeling a sense of accomplishment, purposeful engagement, and a meaningful life narrative enhance emotional well-being.

Emotional wealth is an essential aspect of holistic well-being, encompassing resilience, self-awareness, positive relationships, gratitude, self-care, and a sense of purpose. It contributes significantly to overall happiness, fulfillment, and quality of life.

"I'd rather have roses on my table than diamonds on my neck."

— *Emma Goldman*

III. Principles of Wealth Mastery

A. **Karma Yoga:** The Path to Selfless Action and Abundance

Imagine a life where every action you take is not driven by personal gain or desire for recognition but by a genuine desire to contribute positively to the world. That's the essence of Karma Yoga. It's about performing our duties with dedication and excellence, without being attached to the outcomes.

When we embrace selfless action, we tap into a wellspring of abundance that goes beyond material wealth. This abundance comes from the joy of giving, the satisfaction of making a difference, and the deep sense of purpose that arises from serving others.

Karma Yoga teaches us to let go of the need for validation or control over results. Instead, we focus on doing what's right and what's needed, trusting that the universe will take care of the rest. This mindset frees us from stress and anxiety, allowing us to experience inner peace and contentment.

Practicing Karma Yoga doesn't mean neglecting our own needs or responsibilities. It's about finding a balance between self-care and service to others. By cultivating an abundance mindset rooted in gratitude, compassion, and generosity, we attract positive energy and opportunities into our lives.

Ultimately, Karma Yoga shows us that the path to abundance is paved with selfless actions, a mindset of abundance, and a heart full of love and compassion. It's a journey of spiritual growth, inner richness, and profound fulfillment that leads to a life of true abundance in every sense.

B. Dharma: Aligning Wealth with Duty and Responsibility
Dharma guiding us to align our wealth with a sense of duty and responsibility.
-In simple terms, Dharma refers to living in accordance with moral and ethical principles. When it comes to wealth, Dharma teaches us to acquire and use it in ways that benefit not just ourselves but also others and the world around us.
-One aspect of Dharma is fulfilling our responsibilities and obligations towards our family, community, and society. This includes providing for our loved ones,

supporting those in need, and contributing positively to the well-being of society as a whole.

-Another aspect is using our wealth wisely and ethically. This means earning money through honest means, avoiding exploitation or harm in business dealings, and making responsible financial decisions that consider the long-term impact on others and the environment.

-Dharma also emphasizes the importance of generosity and sharing. It encourages us to use our wealth to help those less fortunate, support charitable causes, and contribute to the common good.

By aligning wealth with Dharma, we not only create a more just and equitable society but also experience a deeper sense of
fulfillment and purpose. It's about recognizing that wealth comes with responsibilities and using it as a tool for positive change and collective well-being.

Karma can totally be wiped out by dhar

C. Detachment: Liberating Wealth from the Bonds of Attachment

Imagine a life where your worth isn't tied to what you own or how much money you have. That's what detachment from wealth means. It's about finding true freedom and fulfillment by letting go of the constant need for more and the anxiety that comes with it.

1- Understanding Attachment: We'll dive into why we often link our happiness and identity to our wealth and possessions. Understanding this can help us see how attachment limits our ability to experience true joy and peace.

2- Inner Wealth: We'll discuss the concept of inner wealth - qualities like gratitude, compassion, and resilience that bring lasting happiness. Cultivating these qualities is key to finding contentment beyond material things.

3- Practical Detachment: I'll share practical tips and mindfulness practices to help you detach from the pressure to constantly acquire more. This might involve mindful spending, simplifying your life, and focusing on experiences rather than possessions.

4- Abundance Mindset: We'll explore shifting from a mindset of scarcity and lack to one of abundance and gratitude. When we see the abundance already present in our lives, we're less likely to feel the need for excessive wealth.

5- True Freedom: Ultimately, detachment leads to freedom - freedom from stress, comparison, and the never-ending pursuit of more. It allows us to appreciate what we have and find joy in the simple thing

1-Understanding Attachment:

(A)Identity and Validation: Many individuals equate their financial status and possessions with their self-worth and social status. This attachment to wealth can stem from societal expectations, cultural influences, and personal beliefs about success and happiness.

(B)Fear of Loss: Attachment to wealth is often fueled by a fear of loss or scarcity mindset. People may worry about losing their wealth, status, or lifestyle, leading to anxiety, stress, and a constant need to accumulate more to feel secure.

(C)Comparison and Social Pressure: In a world where success is often measured by material wealth, individuals may feel pressure to keep up with others or maintain a certain image of success. This can create a cycle of comparison, dissatisfaction, and striving for more.

(D)Emotional Fulfillment: The belief that material possessions and wealth will bring happiness and fulfillment is a common misconception. This section highlights the importance of recognizing that true fulfillment comes from within, through meaningful relationships, personal growth, and a sense of purpose.

(E)Impact on Well-Being: Attachment to wealth can have negative effects on mental and emotional well-being, such as increased stress, dissatisfaction, and a lack of contentment. It can also strain relationships and lead to a constant pursuit of external validation and approval.

2-Inner Wealth:

(A)Gratitude: Inner wealth involves cultivating a sense of gratitude for what we have in life, appreciating the blessings, experiences, and relationships that bring us joy and fulfillment.

(B)Compassion: It includes having compassion for ourselves and others, showing empathy, kindness, and understanding in our interactions, and contributing positively to the well-being of those around us.

(C)Resilience: Inner wealth encompasses resilience, the ability to bounce back from setbacks, adversity, and challenges with strength, determination, and a positive mindset.

(D)Self-Awareness: It involves self-awareness, understanding our strengths, weaknesses, values, and emotions, and striving for personal growth, authenticity, and self-improvement.

(E)Mindfulness: Inner wealth includes practicing mindfulness, being present in the moment, cultivating inner peace, and reducing stress by focusing on the here and now rather than dwelling on the past or worrying about the future.

(F)Purpose and Meaning: It encompasses finding purpose and meaning in life, pursuing goals and activities that align with our values and passions, and experiencing a sense of fulfillment and satisfaction from contributing to something greater than ourselves.

(G)Love and Connection: Inner wealth involves nurturing loving and meaningful relationships, fostering connections with others based on trust, mutual respect, and support, and experiencing the joy of giving and receiving love.

(H)Authenticity: It includes being true to ourselves, living in alignment with our values, beliefs, and convictions, and expressing our true selves authentically and courageously. Overall, inner wealth is about cultivating a rich inner life filled with gratitude, compassion, resilience, self-awareness, mindfulness, purpose, love, connection, authenticity, and other qualities that contribute to our well-being, happiness, and sense of fulfillment. It forms the foundation for a meaningful and fulfilling life, independent of external circumstances or material possessions.

3-Practical Detachment:
(A)Mindful Consumption: It involves being mindful of our spending habits and consumer choices, avoiding unnecessary purchases, and focusing on buying only what we truly need or value.

(B)Decluttering: Practical detachment includes decluttering our living spaces and letting go of items that no longer serve a purpose or bring us joy. This helps create a sense of space, clarity, and simplicity in our lives.

(C)Non-Attachment to Outcomes: It means letting go of attachment to specific outcomes or results in our endeavors. Instead of obsessing over success or failure, we focus on doing our best and accepting whatever outcome comes with equanimity.

(D)Gratitude Practice: Practical detachment involves cultivating a practice of gratitude, appreciating what we have rather than constantly desiring more. This shifts our focus from scarcity to abundance and reduces the need for excessive accumulation.

(E)Investing in Experiences: It includes prioritizing experiences over material possessions, investing in meaningful activities, adventures, and relationships that enrich our lives and bring lasting fulfillment.

(F)Embracing Impermanence: Practical detachment encourages us to embrace the impermanence of life and the transient nature of material wealth. This perspective helps us let go of attachment to possessions and enjoy the present moment more fully.

(G)Setting Boundaries: It involves setting healthy boundaries with material desires, external pressures, and societal expectations, choosing to live in alignment with our values and priorities rather than external influences.

(H)Inner Fulfillment: Practical detachment ultimately leads to inner fulfillment and peace, as we become less reliant on external factors for our happiness and contentment. We find joy and satisfaction in simple pleasures, meaningful connections, and inner growth.

Overall, practical detachment is about simplifying our lives, letting go of attachment to material things, and finding true freedom and fulfillment within ourselves and our experiences rather than external possessions or achievements.

4-Abundance Mindset:

(A) Gratitude: It starts with being grateful for what we have rather than focusing on what we lack. This mindset shift allows us to see abundance in our lives, whether it's in relationships, opportunities, or resources.

(B) Positivity: An abundance mindset is about seeing the glass as half full rather than half empty. It's about approaching challenges with optimism and believing that setbacks are temporary and can lead to growth.

(C) Opportunity-Oriented: Instead of dwelling on scarcity or competition, an abundance mindset looks for opportunities to collaborate, innovate, and create win-win situations where everyone can benefit.

(D) Generosity: It involves being generous with our time, resources, and knowledge, trusting that giving freely will lead to abundance coming back to us in various forms.

(E) Lack of Fear: With an abundance mindset, we let go of fear and scarcity-based thinking. We believe in our ability to create abundance and success, and we don't let fear hold us back from taking risks or pursuing our dreams.

(F) Solution-Oriented: When faced with challenges, an abundance mindset focuses on finding creative solutions rather than dwelling on problems or limitations. It encourages a proactive and resourceful approach to life.

(G) Belief in Abundance: At its core, an abundance mindset is about believing that there is more than enough to go around for everyone. It's a belief in the infinite possibilities and potential for growth and abundance in all areas of life.

By cultivating an abundance mindset, we can attract positive experiences, opportunities, and relationships into our lives, leading to greater fulfillment, success, and happiness.

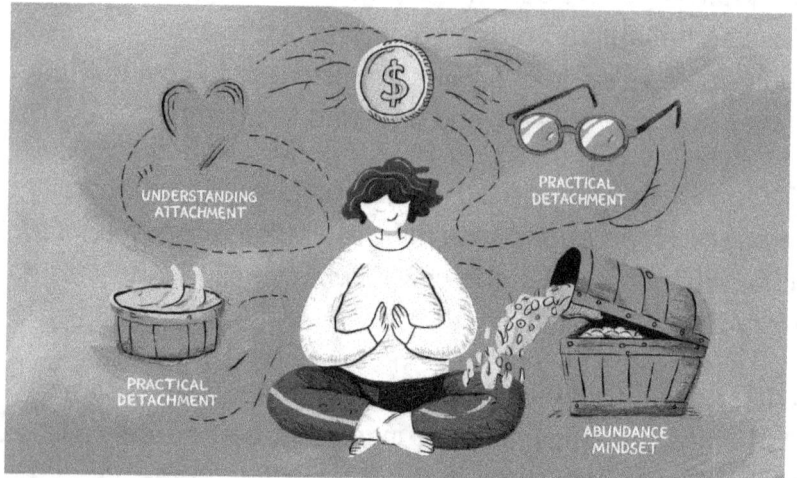

"Risk more than others think is safe. Care more than others think is wise. Dream more than others think is practical. Expect more than others think is possible."

5-True Freedom:

(A)Freedom from External Pressures: True freedom is being free from external pressures, expectations, and societal norms that dictate how we should live or what we should achieve. It's about living authentically, according to our own values and desires, without feeling constrained by outside influences.

(B)Freedom from Fear: It's also about letting go of fear - fear of failure, rejection, judgment, or the unknown. True freedom means facing challenges with courage, embracing uncertainty, and trusting in our ability to navigate life's ups and downs.

(C)Freedom from Attachment: True freedom involves detaching ourselves from attachments to material possessions, outcomes, or identities. It's recognizing that our worth and happiness aren't dependent on external factors but come from within.

(D)Freedom to Choose: It's having the freedom to make choices that align with our values and aspirations, whether it's in our careers, relationships, lifestyles, or personal growth. It's about owning our decisions and taking responsibility for our lives.

(E)Freedom to Be Yourself: True freedom is the ability to express ourselves authentically, without fear of judgment or rejection. It's embracing our uniqueness, quirks, and imperfections, and allowing others to do the same.

(F)Inner Peace and Contentment: Ultimately, true freedom is about finding inner peace and contentment, regardless of external circumstances. It's experiencing a deep sense of fulfillment, joy, and purpose that comes from living in alignment with our true selves.

By striving for true freedom, we can live more fully, authentically, and joyfully, creating a life that reflects our values, passions, and deepest aspirations.

D.Generosity: Sharing Wealth for Collective Prosperity
(A)Sharing Wealth: Generosity involves sharing our material wealth, money, and possessions with others who may be in need or less fortunate. It's about giving without expecting anything in return and sharing our abundance to improve the lives of others.

(B)Resources and Opportunities: Generosity extends beyond money and includes sharing resources, opportunities, and privileges that we have access to. It's about creating opportunities for others to succeed and thrive, whether it's through mentorship, networking, or providing access to education and opportunities.

(C)Time and Energy: Generosity also encompasses giving our time, energy, and efforts to support others and contribute to causes that we believe in. It's about volunteering, helping those in need, and using our skills and talents for the greater good.

(D)Kindness and Compassion: Generosity is rooted in kindness and compassion towards others. It's about being empathetic, understanding, and supportive, and showing care and concern for the well-being of others.

(E)Creating Collective Prosperity: Ultimately, generosity is about creating collective prosperity and well-being for everyone. It's about recognizing that when we share and support each other, we all benefit and contribute to a more compassionate, equitable, and thriving community and world.

By practicing generosity, we not only make a positive impact on the lives of others but also experience a sense of fulfillment, connection, and purpose that comes from giving and making a difference in the world.

"We do not have to be smarter than the rest, we have to be more disciplined than the rest."

E. Discipline: Cultivating Financial Integrity and Management

(A) Budgeting: Discipline involves creating and sticking to a budget that outlines our income, expenses, savings, and investments. It helps us track where our money goes and ensures that we allocate funds wisely based on our priorities and financial goals.

(B) Saving and Investing: Discipline also includes developing a habit of saving a portion of our income regularly and investing it wisely for future growth and financial security. It's about prioritizing long-term financial stability over short-term gratification.

(C) Avoiding Debt: Discipline in financial management means avoiding unnecessary debt and managing existing debts responsibly. It involves making informed decisions about borrowing, using credit cards wisely, and paying off debts in a timely manner to avoid interest charges.

(D) Financial Goals: Discipline includes setting clear financial goals, such as saving for a home, retirement, education, or travel, and creating a plan to achieve these goals. It involves making consistent progress towards our goals through disciplined saving, investing, and spending habits.

(E)Emergency Fund: Discipline also entails building an emergency fund to cover unexpected expenses or financial setbacks. It's about being prepared for unforeseen circumstances and having a financial cushion to fall back on without relying on credit or loans.

(F)Mindful Spending: Discipline involves practicing mindful spending, avoiding impulsive purchases, and distinguishing between needs and wants. It's about making conscious choices about how we use our money and prioritizing spending on essentials and meaningful experiences.

(G)Regular Review: Discipline in financial management includes regularly reviewing and adjusting our financial plan and goals based on changing circumstances, income, expenses, and investment performance. It's about staying proactive and adaptable in managing our finances.

Overall, discipline in financial integrity and management is about adopting a responsible and structured approach to handling money, making informed decisions, and working towards financial stability, security, and prosperity in the long run.

F. Knowledge: Empowering Wealth Creation through Financial Literacy

(A) Understanding Finances: Financial literacy starts with understanding basic financial concepts like budgeting, saving, investing, debt management, and retirement planning. It's about knowing how money works and how to make it work for you.

(B) Making Informed Decisions: With financial literacy, you can make informed decisions about your money. This includes knowing how to compare financial products, like bank accounts or investment options, and choosing the ones that align with your goals and risk tolerance.

(C) Building Wealth: Financial literacy empowers you to build wealth over time. This might involve setting financial goals, creating a budget, saving regularly, investing wisely, and managing debt effectively. It's about taking steps to grow your financial resources and achieve financial independence.

(D) Protecting Yourself: Financial literacy also includes understanding how to protect yourself financially. This can involve having insurance coverage, creating an emergency fund, and planning for unexpected expenses or life events that could impact your finances.

(E) Planning for the Future: Financial literacy helps you plan for the future, whether it's saving for retirement, funding your children's education, or buying a home. It's about thinking ahead and making financial decisions that support your long-term goals and aspirations.

(F) Staying Informed: Being financially literate means staying informed about changes in the financial landscape, economic trends, and new opportunities or risks that could affect your finances. It's about continuous learning and adapting your financial strategies as needed.

Overall, financial literacy is about empowering yourself with the knowledge and skills to manage your money effectively, build wealth, protect your financial well-being, and achieve your financial goals. It's a tool for empowerment and creating a secure and prosperous financial future.

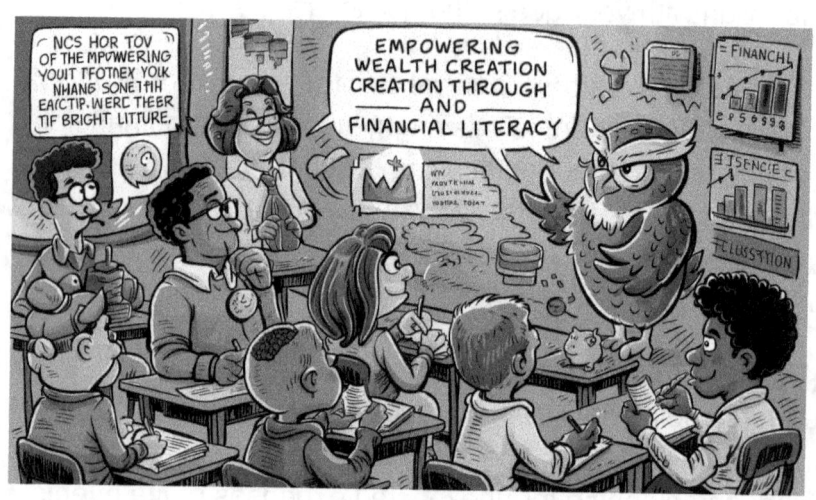

IV. Wealth and Happiness

A. Beyond Materialism: Finding True Happiness in Wealth

Once upon a time, there were two friends, Darshan and Ashish, who lived in the same neighborhood. Darshan was a successful businessman, owning multiple companies and living in a luxurious mansion. He had all the material wealth one could desire – fancy cars, designer clothes, and a big bank account. On the surface, he seemed to have it all.

On the other hand, Ashish was a doctor at a local hospital. He lived in a modest apartment and didn't have a lot of money. However, He had a loving family, close friends, and a deep sense of fulfillment from her work helping children learn and grow.

One day, Darshan and Ashish met for coffee, and Darshan shared how stressed and unfulfilled he felt despite his wealth. He constantly worried about maintaining his businesses, impressing others with his possessions, and never felt truly satisfied. Ashish, on the other hand, radiated happiness and contentment. He talked about the joy of treating patients, the support of his family, and the meaningful relationships he cherished.

As time went on, Darshan realized that while wealth brought comfort and convenience, it didn't guarantee happiness. He saw that Ashish, despite having less material wealth, was much happier because he focused on what truly mattered – love, relationships, and personal fulfillment.

Through their friendship, Darshan learned that true happiness comes from a balance of wealth and non-material factors like relationships, purpose, and inner peace. He started prioritizing time with loved ones, pursuing passions outside of work, and finding joy in simple moments. In doing so, he discovered a deeper sense of happiness that went beyond material possessions.

B. Importance of inner fulfillment and contentment

Inner fulfillment and contentment are like the fuel that keeps our emotional well-being running smoothly. They are the feelings of satisfaction, peace, and happiness that come from within, independent of external circumstances like wealth, status, or material possessions.

When we prioritize inner fulfillment, we focus on things that truly matter to us, such as meaningful relationships, personal growth, and pursuing our passions. This focus allows us to experience a deep sense of satisfaction and contentment, even when facing challenges or setbacks in life.
Having inner fulfillment means being comfortable with who we are, accepting both our strengths and weaknesses, and finding joy in the present moment. It empowers us to navigate life's ups and downs with resilience and a positive outlook, leading to a more fulfilling and meaningful life overall.

In essence, while external achievements and material success can bring temporary happiness, true and lasting contentment comes from cultivating inner fulfillment and aligning our actions with our values and passions.

C. Balancing material prosperity with spiritual well-being

Imagine your life as a garden. Material prosperity is like tending to the outer beauty of the garden – planting colorful flowers, trimming the hedges, and creating a visually appealing space. This represents the tangible aspects of life, such as wealth, career success, and material possessions.

While these things can bring comfort and enjoyment, they alone may not fulfill the deeper needs of the soul.

On the other hand, spiritual well-being is like nurturing the soil of the garden – ensuring it's fertile, nourished, and capable of sustaining healthy growth. This represents the intangible aspects of life, such as inner peace, personal growth, meaningful relationships, and a sense of purpose or connection to something greater, whether it's a spiritual belief, a cause you're passionate about, or a sense of community.

Balancing material prosperity with spiritual well-being means recognizing the importance of both aspects in creating a fulfilling and meaningful life. It involves:

(A)Setting Priorities: Identifying what truly matters to you beyond material success, such as personal values, relationships, health, and personal growth.

(B)Practicing Gratitude: Appreciating and being grateful for what you have, both materially and spiritually, fosters contentment and inner peace.

(C)Mindful Living: Being present in the moment, practicing mindfulness, and cultivating self-awareness can help you align your actions with your values and aspirations.

(D)Self-Care: Taking care of your physical, mental, and emotional well-being is essential for maintaining balance and resilience in the face of life's challenges.

By balancing material prosperity with spiritual well-being, you create a holistic and fulfilling life that encompasses both outer success and inner fulfillment.

> Happiness comes from spiritual wealth, not material wealth... Happiness comes from giving, not getting.
>
> SIR JOHN TEMPLETON

V. Challenges and Obstacles

A. Taming the Greed: Overcoming the Pitfalls of Wealth

Imagine you have a big bowl of your favorite dessert in front of you. At first, it's delicious, and you enjoy every bite. But as you keep eating, you start feeling overly full, maybe even a bit sick. This is similar to how greed works with wealth.

Greed is like an insatiable hunger for more and more, even when you already have plenty. It can lead to unhealthy behaviors like hoarding, selfishness, and a constant desire for more, regardless of the consequences.

"Taming the Greed" means learning to control this desire for excessive wealth and possessions. It involves:

(A) Cultivating Contentment: Being grateful for what you have and finding joy in simple things can help reduce the urge for constant accumulation.

(B) Setting Boundaries: Establishing clear priorities and limits around how much wealth and material possessions you truly need can prevent overindulgence.

(C) Practicing Generosity: Sharing your wealth with others through acts of kindness, charity, and giving back to the community can bring a sense of fulfillment and purpose.

(D)Seeking Balance: Balancing the pursuit of financial success with other aspects of life, such as relationships, personal growth, and well-being, can lead to a more balanced and fulfilling life overall.

(E)Self-Reflection: Regularly reflecting on your values, motivations, and the impact of your actions can help you stay grounded and mindful in your approach to wealth.

By taming greed and overcoming the pitfalls of wealth, you can cultivate a healthier and more fulfilling relationship with money and possessions, leading to greater overall well-being and satisfaction.

B.Conquering Fear: Embracing Resilience in Financial Challenges
Imagine you're on a journey through a dense forest. Along the way, you encounter obstacles like steep hills, deep valleys, and thick bushes blocking your path. These obstacles represent the financial challenges and fears we encounter in life.
"Conquering Fear" means not letting these challenges overwhelm or paralyze you. Instead, it's about embracing resilience – the ability to bounce back and thrive even in the face of adversity. It involves:

(B)1-Facing Fear: Acknowledging and confronting your fears about money, such as fear of failure, loss, or not having enough, is the first step toward overcoming them.

(B)2-Building Financial Literacy: Educating yourself about money management, budgeting, investing, and financial planning can empower you to make informed decisions and navigate challenges more effectively.

(B)3-Creating a Safety Net: Establishing emergency savings, insurance coverage, and a solid financial plan can provide a safety net during tough times and reduce anxiety about the future.

(B)4-Seeking Support: Seeking guidance from financial advisors, mentors, or support networks can offer valuable insights, encouragement, and practical strategies for managing financial challenges.

(B)5-Cultivating Resilience: Developing resilience through practices like mindfulness, self-care, optimism, and adaptability can help you stay strong, focused, and positive during financial setbacks.

By embracing resilience in financial challenges, you can transform fear into courage, uncertainty into opportunity, and setbacks into stepping stones toward a more secure and fulfilling financial future.

VI. Practical Strategies

A. Taking the First Steps: A Beginner's Guide to Entering the Market

What is stock market ?

The Indian stock market is one of the prominent financial markets globally. It comprises various segments and participants, contributing significantly to India's economic growth and development.

Stock Exchanges: The primary stock exchanges in India are the National Stock Exchange (NSE) and the Bombay Stock Exchange (BSE). These exchanges facilitate the buying and selling of securities, including stocks, derivatives, and other financial instruments.

Market Segments: Similar to global markets, the Indian stock market includes segments like equities (stocks), derivatives (futures and options), commodities, currencies (forex), and mutual funds.

Regulatory Framework: The Securities and Exchange Board of India (SEBI) is the regulatory body overseeing the Indian securities market. SEBI regulates stock exchanges, brokers, listed companies, and other market participants to ensure fair and transparent trading practices.

Investor Participation: Indian stock markets attract various types of investors, including retail investors, institutional investors (such as mutual funds, insurance companies, and foreign institutional investors), and foreign investors. The participation of retail investors has increased significantly with the advent of online trading platforms and investor education initiatives.

Stock Market Indices: Key stock market indices in India include the Nifty 50 on the NSE, representing the top 50 companies by market capitalization, and the Sensex on the BSE, comprising the 30 largest and most actively traded stocks.

Market Performance: The Indian stock market's performance is influenced by domestic factors such as economic indicators, corporate earnings, government policies, and global trends, including geopolitical events and international economic conditions.

Investment Opportunities: The Indian stock market offers diverse investment opportunities across sectors such as IT, healthcare, banking, infrastructure, consumer goods, and energy. Investors can choose between long-term investment strategies, trading in derivatives for short-term gains, or investing through mutual funds for portfolio diversification.

Risk and Returns: Like any financial market, the Indian stock market involves risks, including market volatility, regulatory changes, company-specific risks, and global economic uncertainties. Investors need to assess their risk tolerance and investment goals while participating in the stock market.

"A salary is a drug they give you when they want you to forget about your dreams"

Major segments of indian stock market

Mutual Funds: Mutual funds pool money from multiple investors to invest in a diversified portfolio of stocks, bonds, or other securities. In India, mutual funds are managed by asset management companies (AMCs) and offer various schemes catering to different investment objectives and risk profiles.

Equities (Stocks): Equities represent ownership in a company. Investors buy shares of publicly traded companies, and their returns depend on the company's performance and stock price movements. In India, equities are traded on stock exchanges like the NSE and BSE.

Derivatives (Futures and Options): Derivatives are financial contracts whose value is derived from an underlying asset, such as stocks, indices, commodities, or currencies. In India, derivatives trading includes futures contracts (an agreement to buy or sell an asset at a predetermined price on a future date) and options contracts (providing the right, but not the obligation, to buy or sell an asset at a specified price within a certain period).

Commodities: The commodity market in India includes trading in physical commodities like gold, silver, crude oil, agricultural products, and metals. Commodity futures contracts allow investors to speculate on price movements or hedge against price risks.

Currencies (Forex): The foreign exchange market (forex) involves trading currencies from different countries. In India, forex trading occurs in currency pairs such as USD/INR (U.S. Dollar/Indian Rupee) or EUR/INR (Euro/Indian Rupee). Forex trading is influenced by
global economic factors, geopolitical events, and central bank policies.

Mutual Funds

Note:-"First step to enter market without proper knowledge and getting Return on investment which beats inflation,with low risk of losing capital is Mutual funds".

-Compounding:Compounding refers to the process where the value of an investment grows exponentially over time as both the initial principal and the accumulated interest or returns earn further interest or returns. It's often referred to as "interest on interest.

How to select mutual funds?

-Start by clarifying your financial objectives. Are you investing for retirement, education, buying a house, or wealth accumulation? Your goals will influence the type of mutual funds you should consider.
-Determine how much risk you are willing to take. Conservative investors may prefer low-risk funds like debt or money market funds, while aggressive investors may opt for equity funds with higher growth potential but also higher risk.

- Look at a fund's historical performance over different time periods (1 year, 3 years, 5 years, and since inception). Compare its returns with benchmark indices and peer group funds to assess consistency and outperformance.
- Check the expense ratio, which represents the annual fees charged by the fund. Lower expense ratios can enhance your returns over time.
- Assess the fund manager's experience, track record, investment strategy, and decision-making process. A skilled and experienced fund manager can add value to the fund's performance.
- A fund with a substantial AUM and stable size is generally considered more stable and liquid. Asset Under Management (AUM)
- Look at risk measures such as standard deviation, Sharpe ratio, and beta to understand how volatile the fund's returns are and its risk-adjusted performance.
- Review the fund's prospectus, fact sheet, and annual reports to understand its investment objectives, portfolio composition, investment style, and any associated risks.

Types of funds:-

-**Equity Funds:** These invest primarily in stocks and are suitable for long-term growth but come with higher market risk.

-**Debt Funds:** These invest in fixed-income securities like bonds and are considered lower risk compared to equity funds.

-**Hybrid Funds:** Also known as balanced funds, these invest in a mix of equities and debt instruments, offering a balance between growth and stability.

-**Index Funds:** These track a specific market index and aim to replicate its performance.

-**Sector Funds:** These focus on specific sectors like technology, healthcare, or energy, and may have higher risk and volatility.

Note:-"Best of all funds is index fund,as a beginner should start investing in **INDEX** Fund,with moderate risk and good return."

-Mutual fund is an instrument of stock market which helps in creation of wealth in long term.**Time** has more value then **Money** in this segment.
For example:-(A)**500**/month   for **40**yrs =Rs **1crore(2,40,000)**
           (B)**10000**/month for **18**yrs= Rs **1crore(21,60,000)**
               (C)**100000**/month for **6**yr   = Rs **1crore(72,00,000)**

Calculator 1:
- Monthly investment: ₹ 100000
- Expected return rate (p.a): 15%
- Time period: 6 Yr
- Invested amount: ₹72,00,000
- Est. returns: ₹45,11,954
- Total value: ₹1,17,11,954

Calculator 2:
- Monthly investment: ₹ 10000
- Expected return rate (p.a): 15%
- Time period: 18 Yr
- Invested amount: ₹21,60,000
- Est. returns: ₹88,82,553
- Total value: ₹1,10,42,553

Calculator 3:
- Monthly investment: ₹ 500
- Expected return rate (p.a): 15%
- Time period: 40 Yr
- Invested amount: ₹2,40,000
- Est. returns: ₹1,54,61,878
- Total value: ₹1,57,01,878

What is SIP- Systematic Investment Plan ?

SIP allows you to invest a specific amount at regular intervals (e.g., monthly) in mutual funds. This disciplined approach helps in accumulating wealth over time without requiring a large initial investment.

Benefits of SIP

-Rupee Cost Averaging: By investing regularly, you buy more units when prices are low and fewer when prices are high, averaging out the purchase cost.

-Compounding: Regular investments over time can lead to significant growth due to the power of compounding.

-Flexibility: You can start with a small amount, increase or decrease your investment, or even stop it without penalties.

-Discipline: Regular investments instill financial discipline and long-term saving habits.

-Convenience: Automated investments make it easy to invest without the need to time the market.

How to Start a SIP

-Choose a Mutual Fund: Research and select a mutual fund that aligns with your financial goals and risk tolerance.

-Decide the Amount: Determine how much you want to invest regularly.

-Set Up the SIP: Register with a mutual fund provider or through your bank or Demat account. Choose the frequency (monthly, quarterly) and link your bank account for auto-debits.

-Monitor Your Investment: Periodically review your investments to ensure they are on track to meet your goals.

SIP in the Context of Indian Stock Market
In India, SIPs are a popular way to invest in mutual funds. They offer a convenient and systematic way for investors to benefit from the growth potential of equity markets without the need to actively manage their investments.

Types of SIPs

1.Regular SIP

Fixed Amount: You invest a fixed amount at regular intervals (e.g., monthly).
Standard Plan: The most common and straightforward type of SIP, where you decide the amount and the frequency of investment.
2. Flexible SIP

Variable Amount: You can change the investment amount based on your financial situation.
Flexibility: Allows you to invest more when you have surplus funds and less when you need to cut back.

3. Top-up SIP
Incremental Investment: You can increase your investment amount periodically.
Growth-Oriented: Helps in boosting your investment amount in line with your increasing income or savings.

4. Perpetual SIP
No End Date: Continues until you decide to stop it.
Long-Term Commitment: Ideal for long-term investors who prefer to keep investing without having to renew their SIP mandate.

5. Trigger SIP
Conditional Investment: Investments are made based on certain predetermined triggers, such as NAV (Net Asset Value) reaching a specific level, market index movements, or dates.
Strategic: Suitable for investors who want to invest based on market conditions or specific events.

6. SIP with Insurance
Insurance Coverage: Some SIPs come with an insurance cover that offers life insurance benefits.
Dual Benefit: Combines investment with protection, ensuring financial security for your family.

7. Multi-SIP
Multiple Funds: Allows you to invest in multiple mutual funds through a single SIP.

Diversification: Offers the benefit of diversification across different funds and asset classes.

8. Goal-Based SIP
Targeted Investment: Designed to help you achieve specific financial goals such as buying a house, funding education, or retirement planning.
Customized: Tailored investment plans based on the time horizon and financial goals.

9. Step-up SIP
Scheduled Increase: Your SIP amount increases at regular intervals.
Income Growth: Matches your increasing income levels, allowing you to invest more over time.

Note:- **Regular SIP** and **Step-up SIP** are most commonly used as beginner to intermediate in India.

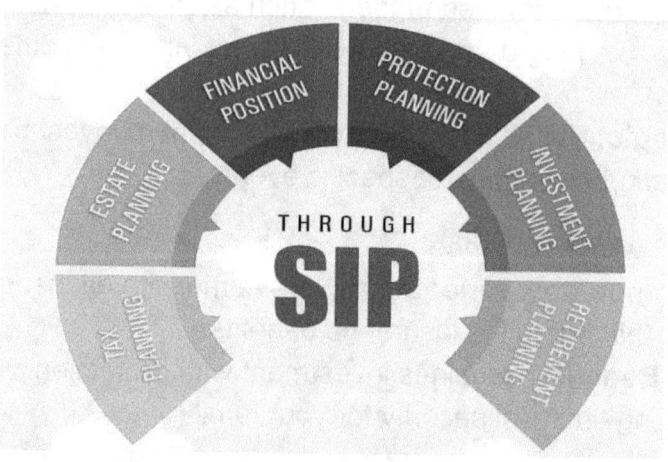

How SIPs Work ?

Selection of Mutual Fund: Choose a mutual fund based on your investment goals, risk tolerance, and time horizon. You can select from various types of funds like equity, debt, or hybrid funds.

Deciding the SIP Amount: Determine the amount you wish to invest regularly. This can be as small as a few hundred rupees or as large as you prefer, depending on the fund's minimum investment requirement.

Setting Up the SIP: You register for the SIP with the mutual fund company or through an intermediary (like a broker or an online platform). You specify the amount, frequency (monthly, quarterly, etc.), and the duration of the SIP.

Automated Investments: Once set up, the SIP amount is automatically deducted from your bank account at the chosen frequency and invested in the selected mutual fund. This continues for the specified period or until you decide to stop or modify the SIP.

Units Allocation: With each SIP installment, you purchase units of the mutual fund based on the prevailing Net Asset Value (NAV) on the date of investment. The NAV fluctuates based on market conditions.

Rupee Cost Averaging: SIPs take advantage of rupee cost averaging, which means you buy more units when prices are low and fewer units when prices are high. Over time, this averages out the cost of your investments and reduces the impact of market volatility.

Compounding: The returns on your investments get reinvested, leading to compounding. This means you earn returns on your initial investment as well as on the returns generated, helping your money grow faster over time.

Flexibility and Convenience: SIPs are flexible. You can increase or decrease the SIP amount, pause it, or stop it altogether without significant penalties. This provides convenience and adaptability to changing financial situations.

Tracking and Monitoring: You can monitor the performance of your SIP through regular account statements provided by the mutual fund company. Online platforms also offer tools to track and analyze your investments.

Redemption: You can redeem your mutual fund units partially or fully at any time, subject to any exit load or redemption fees that might apply. The redemption proceeds are credited to your bank account.

Example

Suppose you decide to invest ₹5,000 monthly in an equity mutual fund through a SIP. Over a year, you invest ₹60,000. Depending on the **NAV** at the time of each investment, you buy different numbers of units each month. If the **NAV** is low, you get more units; if it's high, you get fewer units. Over time, the value of your investment grows based on the performance of the mutual fund and the benefits of **rupee cost averaging and compounding**.

By consistently investing through SIPs, you can build a significant corpus over the long term, aligned with your financial goals and risk appetite.

How Mutual Funds Work ?

Investor Contribution:
-Assume an investor invests ₹10,000 in a mutual fund.
-This money is pooled with funds from other investors, creating a larger investment corpus.

Portfolio Management:
-The fund manager allocates the pooled money across various securities, such as stocks, bonds, and money market instruments, based on the fund's investment strategy.

NAV Calculation:
-At the end of each trading day, the total value of the fund's investments is calculated. If the fund's assets are worth ₹1,00,00,000 and there are 10,000 units outstanding, the NAV per unit would be ₹1,000.

Investment Growth:
-Over time, if the value of the investments increases due to market performance, the NAV will rise. If the fund's assets grow to ₹1,20,00,000, and the number of units remains the same, the NAV will increase to ₹1,200.

Income Distribution:
-The mutual fund may earn dividends from stocks or interest from bonds, which can be reinvested or distributed to investors as income.
-**Redeeming Units:**
If an investor decides to redeem their units when the NAV is ₹1,200, they would receive ₹1,200 for each unit sold, reflecting the growth in the value of their investment.

Systematic Withdrawal Plan (SWP)

A Systematic Withdrawal Plan (SWP) is a financial strategy designed to provide investors with a steady flow of income by systematically redeeming units from their investment portfolio at predetermined intervals. This approach is commonly used with mutual funds but can also be applied to other types of investment accounts. SWP is particularly beneficial for retirees or those seeking regular income without depleting their principal investment too quickly.

How SWP Works:

Fixed Withdrawals: Investors specify a fixed amount they wish to withdraw regularly (monthly, quarterly, or annually). This amount is redeemed from the investment fund.

Flexibility: The withdrawal amount and frequency can often be adjusted to suit the investor's changing financial needs.

Tax Efficiency: In some cases, SWP can offer tax advantages compared to lump-sum withdrawals, as it spreads out the taxable income over time.

Capital Preservation: By withdrawing only a portion of the investment, the remaining balance continues to stay invested, potentially benefiting from market growth and compounding returns.

Considerations:

Withdrawal Rate: It's crucial to set a sustainable withdrawal rate to ensure the investment lasts as long as needed.

Market Performance: The performance of the underlying investment can impact the longevity of the SWP. Poor market conditions might necessitate adjustments to the withdrawal amount.

Fees and Charges: Be aware of any fees associated with withdrawals, as they can erode the overall returns.

How to Apply for a Systematic Withdrawal Plan (SWP)
1. Choose the Right Mutual Fund:
Research and Selection: Select a mutual fund that aligns with your financial goals, risk tolerance, and investment horizon. Look for funds that offer SWP options.

Consultation: Consider consulting with a financial advisor to ensure you choose the right fund for your needs.

2. Open an Account:
KYC Compliance: Ensure you are KYC (Know Your Customer) compliant. This is a mandatory requirement for investing in mutual funds in many countries.

Account Setup: If you do not already have an account with the mutual fund company, you will need to open one. This can usually be done online or by visiting the mutual fund company's office or your bank.

3. Invest in the Mutual Fund:
Initial Investment: Make an initial investment in the chosen mutual fund. This can be done through a lump sum investment or via a Systematic Investment Plan (SIP).

Minimum Balance: Ensure that you have the required minimum balance in your mutual fund account to start an SWP.

4. Submit the SWP Application Form:

Obtain the Form: Obtain the SWP application form from the mutual fund company's website, office, or your financial advisor.

Fill in Details: Complete the form with the necessary details such as your name, mutual fund account number, the amount you wish to withdraw, the frequency of withdrawals (monthly, quarterly, etc.), and the start date for the SWP.

Bank Details: Provide your bank account details where the SWP payments will be credited.

5. Choose the Withdrawal Amount and Frequency:

Fixed Amount: Decide the fixed amount you want to withdraw at each interval.

Frequency: Choose the frequency of withdrawals, such as monthly, quarterly, semi-annually, or annually.

6. Submit the Form:

Submission: Submit the completed SWP application form to the mutual fund company. This can often be done online, by mail, or in person at the mutual fund company's office or your bank.

Confirmation: Once the form is submitted, you will receive a confirmation from the mutual fund company. This confirmation will include the details of your SWP, such as the withdrawal amount, frequency, and start date.

7. Monitor Your SWP:

Regular Updates: Keep track of your SWP by regularly reviewing your mutual fund statements. Ensure that the withdrawals are happening as per the plan.

Adjustments: If your financial situation changes, you may need to adjust the withdrawal amount or frequency. Most mutual fund companies allow you to modify or cancel your SWP by submitting a request.

Who Can Benefit from a Systematic Withdrawal Plan (SWP)

A Systematic Withdrawal Plan (SWP) is a versatile financial tool that can benefit a wide range of investors. Here are some groups who can particularly benefit from an SWP:

1. Retirees:

Regular Income: SWP provides a predictable and steady income stream, which is essential for retirees who need to meet their daily living expenses without worrying about depleting their savings too quickly.

Flexibility: Retirees can adjust the withdrawal amount based on their changing financial needs and circumstances.

2. Individuals Seeking Passive Income:

Supplementary Income: Those who are not yet retired but seek an additional income stream can use SWP to supplement their earnings.

Financial Independence: SWP can be part of a strategy to achieve financial independence by generating a regular cash flow from investments.

3. Parents Planning for Children's Education:

Educational Expenses: Parents can use SWP to fund their children's education expenses by withdrawing a fixed amount regularly.

Long-term Planning: By starting early, parents can ensure a steady flow of funds for school fees, college tuition, and other educational costs.

4. Individuals with Irregular Income:
Stability: For individuals with fluctuating or irregular incomes (e.g., freelancers, consultants), SWP can provide a stable cash flow to cover regular expenses.

Budget Management: It helps in better budgeting and financial planning by providing a consistent income.

5. Investors with Low-Risk Tolerance:
Capital Preservation: Investors who prefer a conservative approach and want to preserve their capital while still drawing an income can benefit from SWP.

Market Risk Mitigation: Regular withdrawals help in reducing the impact of market volatility on their income.

6. Tax-Sensitive Investors:

Tax Efficiency: In some jurisdictions, SWP can be more tax-efficient compared to lump-sum withdrawals, as the gains are spread over multiple financial years, potentially resulting in lower tax liability.

Tax Planning: Investors can strategically plan their withdrawals to minimize tax implications.

7. Charitable Giving:
Philanthropy: Individuals who wish to make regular charitable donations can use SWP to systematically fund their contributions without impacting their financial stability.

Structured Giving: It allows for a structured and planned approach to philanthropy.

8. Investors in the Distribution Phase:
Wealth Distribution: Those in the distribution phase of their investment lifecycle can use SWP to systematically convert their investments into income.

Legacy Planning: It helps in ensuring that their wealth lasts through their lifetime and can be efficiently passed on to their heirs.

Merits and Demerits of Systematic Withdrawal Plan (SWP)

Merits of SWP:
Regular Income Stream:
Steady Cash Flow: SWP provides a predictable and regular income, which is beneficial for retirees or anyone seeking a steady cash flow.

Financial Planning: Helps in better financial planning by ensuring a fixed amount is available at regular intervals.

Flexibility:
Customizable Withdrawals: Investors can choose the withdrawal amount and frequency (monthly, quarterly, annually) based on their needs.

Adjustability: The withdrawal amount and frequency can be adjusted or stopped as per changing financial circumstances.

Tax Efficiency:

Tax Benefits: In some jurisdictions, the withdrawals through SWP might be taxed at a lower rate compared to lump-sum withdrawals. The capital gains tax is spread over multiple financial years.

Tax Planning: Allows for strategic tax planning, potentially reducing the overall tax liability.

Market Risk Mitigation:
Volatility Management: By withdrawing regularly, investors can mitigate the impact of market volatility on their investments.

Avoids Lump-Sum Withdrawals: Prevents the need to withdraw a large sum during market downturns, which could deplete the investment faster.

Capital Preservation:
Principal Protection: Helps in preserving the principal amount as only a portion of the investment is withdrawn periodically.

Growth Potential: The remaining invested amount continues to earn returns, potentially growing over time.

Convenience:
Automated Process: Once set up, SWP is automated, providing convenience and ease of managing finances.

No Need for Market Timing: Investors do not need to worry about timing the market to make withdrawals.

Demerits of SWP:

Market Dependency:
Variable Returns: The performance of the underlying investments affects the SWP. Poor market performance can impact the longevity and sustainability of the SWP.

Potential Capital Erosion: In adverse market conditions, there is a risk of capital erosion if the withdrawals exceed the returns generated.

Withdrawal Rate Risk:
Unsustainable Withdrawals: If the withdrawal rate is too high, it can deplete the investment faster than anticipated.

Longevity Risk: There is a risk that the funds may not last for the intended period, especially if the withdrawals are not carefully planned.

Fees and Charges:
Transaction Costs: Frequent withdrawals may incur transaction costs or fees, which can reduce the overall returns.

Management Fees: Mutual funds charge management fees, which can eat into the returns over time.

Inflation Risk:
Purchasing Power: Fixed withdrawal amounts may not keep pace with inflation, potentially reducing the purchasing power over time.

Need for Adjustments: Investors may need to periodically adjust the withdrawal amount to account for inflation.

Complexity in Taxation:
Tax Compliance: Managing and understanding the tax implications of each withdrawal can be complex and may require professional advice.

Documentation: Requires careful documentation and tracking of withdrawals for tax reporting purposes.

Reduced Growth Potential:
Lower Compounding: Regular withdrawals can reduce the compounding effect on the remaining investment.

Opportunity Cost: The withdrawn amount no longer earns returns, potentially reducing the overall growth of the investment portfolio.

"How many millionaires do you know who have become wealthy by investing in savings accounts?"

Total investment	₹ 5000000	Total investment	₹ 5000000	Total investment	₹ 5000000
Withdrawal per month	₹ 25000	Withdrawal per month	₹ 25000	Withdrawal per month	₹ 25000
Expected return rate (p.a)	12 %	Expected return rate (p.a)	12 %	Expected return rate (p.a)	12 %
Time period	5 Yr	Time period	10 Yr	Time period	20 Yr
Total investment	₹50,00,000	Total investment	₹50,00,000	Total investment	₹50,00,000
Total withdrawal	₹15,00,000	Total withdrawal	₹30,00,000	Total withdrawal	₹60,00,000
Final value	₹68,03,177	Final value	₹99,80,990	Final value	₹2,54,51,189

Total investment	₹ 5000000	Total investment	₹ 5000000	Total investment	₹ 5000000
Withdrawal per month	₹ 50000	Withdrawal per month	₹ 50000	Withdrawal per month	₹ 50000
Expected return rate (p.a)	12 %	Expected return rate (p.a)	12 %	Expected return rate (p.a)	12 %
Time period	5 Yr	Time period	10 Yr	Time period	20 Yr
Total investment	₹50,00,000	Total investment	₹50,00,000	Total investment	₹50,00,000
Total withdrawal	₹30,00,000	Total withdrawal	₹60,00,000	Total withdrawal	₹1,20,00,000
Final value	₹47,94,845	Final value	₹44,32,739	Final value	₹28,70,912

Advantages of Mutual Funds

-Diversification: Mutual funds invest in a wide variety of securities, which helps spread risk. This diversification can reduce the impact of any single security's poor performance on the overall portfolio.

-Professional Management: Funds are managed by experienced and skilled fund managers who make investment decisions based on research and analysis. This can be particularly beneficial for investors who lack the time or expertise to manage their own investments.

-Liquidity: Open-ended mutual funds provide high liquidity, allowing investors to buy or sell units at any time at the current NAV. This makes it easy to access invested funds when needed.

-Convenience: Investing in mutual funds is straightforward and does not require significant investment knowledge. Investors can start with small amounts and take advantage of systematic investment plans (SIPs) to invest regularly.

-Affordability: Mutual funds allow investors to participate in a diversified portfolio with relatively small amounts of money. This makes them accessible to a broad range of investors.

-Economies of Scale: Because mutual funds pool money from many investors, they can buy and sell securities in larger volumes, often at better prices than individual investors can achieve.

-Variety of Options: There are many types of mutual funds available, catering to different investment objectives, risk tolerances, and time horizons. Investors can choose funds that align with their financial goals.

-**Transparency:** Mutual funds are regulated and required to provide regular updates on their holdings, performance, and fees. This transparency helps investors make informed decisions.

Disadvantages of Mutual Funds

-**Fees and Expenses:** Mutual funds charge management fees and other expenses that can eat into returns. Some funds also charge sales loads (commissions) when you buy or sell shares. These costs can add up over time.

-**Lack of Control:** Investors in mutual funds have no direct control over the individual securities the fund manager chooses to buy or sell. This can be a disadvantage for those who prefer a hands-on approach to investing.

-**Potential for Lower Returns:** While professional management can be an advantage, it does not guarantee higher returns. Some actively managed funds may underperform compared to index funds or other investment strategies.

-**Tax Implications:** Investors may be subject to capital gains taxes when the fund manager sells securities at a profit, even if they haven't sold their own mutual fund shares. This can lead to unexpected tax liabilities.

-**Market Risk:** Like all investments, mutual funds are subject to market risks. The value of the fund's portfolio can fluctuate based on market conditions, potentially leading to losses.

-**Dilution:** Diversification can sometimes lead to over-diversification, where the impact of successful investments is diluted by the less successful ones. This can result in average performance rather than strong returns.

-**Performance Variability:** The performance of mutual funds can vary widely. Not all funds perform well, and past performance is not indicative of future results. Investors must research and select funds carefully.

-**Minimum Investment Requirements:** Some mutual funds have minimum investment requirements, which might be a barrier for small investors. While many funds have low minimums, some specialized funds may require larger initial investments.

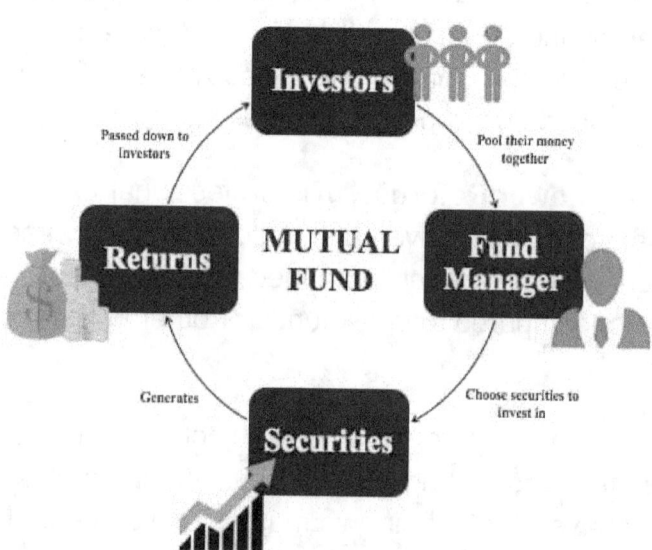

EXAMPLES:-

SIP	Lumpsum	
Monthly investment	₹	500
Expected return rate (p.a)		15%
Time period		40 Yr
Invested amount		₹2,40,000
Est. returns		₹1,54,61,878
Total value		₹1,57,01,878

Monthly investment	₹	5000
Expected return rate (p.a)		15%
Time period		40 Yr
Invested amount		₹24,00,000
Est. returns		₹15,46,18,777
Total value		₹15,70,18,777

Monthly investment	₹	10000
Expected return rate (p.a)		15%
Time period		40 Yr
Invested amount		₹48,00,000
Est. returns		₹30,92,37,555
Total value		₹31,40,37,555

THE 15X15X15 RULE

Monthly investment	₹ 15000
Expected return rate (p.a)	15%
Time period	15 Yr

Invested amount	₹27,00,000
Est. returns	₹74,52,946
Total value	₹1,01,52,946

EQUITIES (Stocks)

Equities, commonly referred to as stocks, represent ownership shares in a company. When you purchase a stock, you become a shareholder, owning a portion of the company's assets and earnings. Stocks are a fundamental component of the stock market and are traded on exchanges such as the National Stock Exchange (NSE) and Bombay Stock Exchange (BSE) in India.

Benefits of Investing in Equities

-**Potential for High Returns:** Historically, equities have provided higher returns compared to other investment vehicles over the long term.
-**Dividends:** Shareholders may receive periodic dividends, which are a portion of the company's profits distributed to investors.
-**Ownership:** Being a shareholder means you have a stake in the company's growth and success.

Risks of Investing in Equities

-**Market Volatility:** Stock prices can be highly volatile and subject to market fluctuations.
-**Company Performance:** The value of stocks depends on the company's performance, which can be influenced by management decisions, market conditions, and other factors.
-**Economic Factors:** Broader economic factors, including interest rates, inflation, and political events, can impact stock prices.

Stock Market Indices

-Nifty 50: A benchmark index of the NSE, comprising 50 of the largest and most liquid stocks.

-SENSEX: The benchmark index of the BSE, representing 30 of the largest and most actively traded stocks.

Trading Strategies

-Long-Term Investing: Holding stocks for an extended period to benefit from the company's growth and compounding returns.

-Short-Term Trading: Buying and selling stocks within short time frames to capitalize on market movements.

-Dividend Investing: Focusing on stocks that provide regular dividend income.

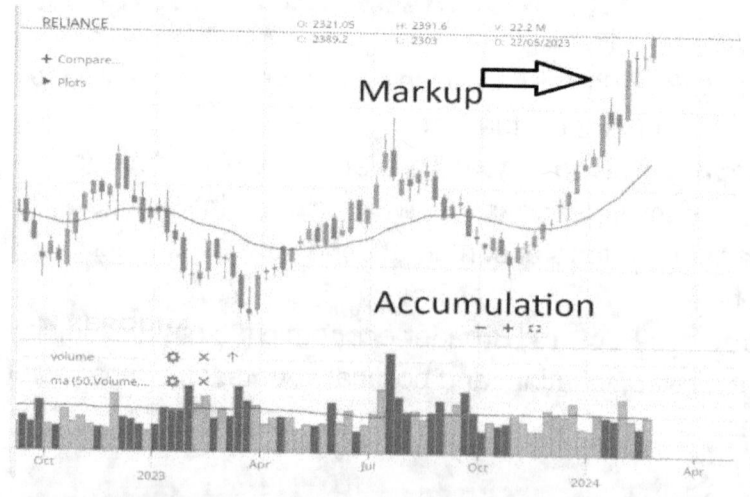

Steps to Begin Investing in Equities

-Research and Education: Understand the basics of the stock market and conduct thorough research on companies and industries.

-Open a Demat and Trading Account: Necessary for buying and holding stocks electronically.

-Set Investment Goals: Define your financial objectives, risk tolerance, and investment horizon.

-Diversify Your Portfolio: Spread your investments across different sectors and companies to mitigate risk.

-Monitor and Review: Regularly review your portfolio and stay informed about market trends and company performance.

NOTE:- Two main types of analysis to enter stocks/cash/delhivery /equity and more are-

    (1)-**Fundamental analysis**
    (2)-**Technical analysis**

-**Fundamental analysis:-**Fundamental analysis is a cornerstone of value investing, where the goal is to purchase stocks that are undervalued relative to their intrinsic value and hold them until the market recognizes their true worth.
    Example-Stocks
        -Long term investing,etc.

-**Technical analysis:-**Technical analysis is a powerful tool for traders who seek to understand and predict market movements based on historical data and market psychology. It is often used in conjunction with fundamental analysis to provide a comprehensive view of a Stocks potential.
    Examples-FnO(Futures and options)
        -Swing trading
        -Intraday etc.

The stock market is a device to transfer money from the impatient to the patient. -Warren Buffett

Fundamental analysis

-Economic Analysis:
$)**Macroeconomic Indicators:** Factors such as GDP growth, inflation, interest rates, and employment rates that affect the overall economy.

$)**Industry Analysis:** Evaluating the industry in which a company operates, including market size, competition, regulatory environment, and growth prospects.

-Financial Statement Analysis:
$)**Income Statement:** Assesses the company's profitability over a specific period by examining revenue, expenses, and net income.

$)**Balance Sheet:** Provides a snapshot of the company's financial position at a specific point in time, including assets, liabilities, and shareholders' equity.

$)**Cash Flow Statement:** Analyzes the company's cash inflows and outflows from operating, investing, and financing activities.

-Financial Ratios:
$)**Profitability Ratios:** Measure the company's ability to generate profit relative to revenue, assets, and equity (e.g., net profit margin, return on assets, return on equity).
$)**Liquidity Ratios:** Assess the company's ability to meet short-term obligations (e.g., current ratio, quick ratio).
$)**Solvency Ratios:** Evaluate the company's long-term financial stability (e.g., debt-to-equity ratio, interest coverage ratio).

$)Efficiency Ratios: Indicate how well the company uses its assets and liabilities to generate sales and maximize profit (e.g., asset turnover ratio, inventory turnover ratio).

-Qualitative Analysis:

$)Management: Evaluating the quality, experience, and track record of the company's management team.

$)Business Model: Understanding the company's business model, competitive advantage, and revenue streams.

$)Corporate Governance: Assessing the company's governance practices, board structure, and ethical standards.

-Intrinsic Value Calculation:

$)Discounted Cash Flow (DCF) Analysis: Estimates the present value of future cash flows expected from the company.

$)Comparable Company Analysis: Compares the company's valuation metrics with those of similar companies in the industry.

$)Dividend Discount Model (DDM): Values the company based on the present value of expected future dividends.

"I make no attempt to forecast the market—my efforts are devoted to finding undervalued securities." **-Warren Buffett**

Steps in Conducting Fundamental Analysis

-**Gather Information:** Collect data from financial statements, industry reports, and economic indicators.

-**Analyze Financial Statements:** Examine the income statement, balance sheet, and cash flow statement to understand the company's financial health.

-**Evaluate Financial Ratios:** Calculate and interpret key financial ratios to assess profitability, liquidity, solvency, and efficiency.

-**Assess Qualitative Factors:** Consider management quality, business model, competitive position, and corporate governance.

-**Determine Intrinsic Value:** Use valuation models to estimate the stock's intrinsic value based on future cash flows, dividends, or comparable companies.

-**Make Investment Decision:** Compare the intrinsic value with the current market price to decide whether the stock is undervalued, overvalued, or fairly valued.

Benefits of Fundamental Analysis:

-**Long-Term Perspective:** Helps investors identify stocks with strong fundamentals and growth potential.
-**Informed Decision-Making:** Provides a comprehensive understanding of a company's financial health and business prospects.
-**Risk Management:** Enables investors to identify potential risks and make more informed investment choices.

-Fundamental analysis to be considered are:-

($)**Market Cap:**-Market capitalization, often referred to as market cap, is a measure of a company's total value as determined by the stock market. It is calculated by multiplying the current share price by the 0total number of outstanding shares. Market cap helps investors understand the relative size of a company compared to others in the market and categorize companies into different tiers.

($)**P/E Ratio:**-The Price-to-Earnings (P/E) ratio is a commonly used metric in fundamental analysis to assess a company's valuation relative to its earnings. It indicates how much investors are willing to pay for each dollar of earnings.

The P/E ratio is calculated by dividing the current market price of a stock by its earnings per share (EPS).

($)P/B Ratio:- The Price-to-Book (P/B) ratio is a financial metric used to compare a company's market value to its book value. It is calculated by dividing the current market price per share by the book value per share (BVPS). This ratio helps investors assess whether a stock is undervalued or overvalued by comparing the market's valuation of a company to its actual net asset value.

($)Industry P/E:- The Industry P/E (Price-to-Earnings) ratio is a valuation metric that provides an average P/E ratio for all the companies within a particular industry. This ratio helps investors gauge the relative valuation of a company compared to its industry peers. By comparing a company's P/E ratio to the industry average, investors can determine if the company is overvalued, undervalued, or fairly valued relative to other companies in the same sector.

($)Debt-to-Equity (D/E) ratio:- The Debt-to-Equity (D/E) ratio is a financial metric used to evaluate a company's financial leverage by comparing its total liabilities to its shareholder equity. This ratio provides insight into the extent to which a company is financing its operations through debt versus wholly-owned funds.

($)Return on Equity (ROE):- Return on Equity (ROE) is a financial ratio that measures a company's ability to generate profits from its shareholders' equity. It indicates how efficiently a company is using the money invested by its shareholders to generate earnings. ROE is a key metric for assessing the profitability and financial performance of a company.

($)Earnings per Share (EPS):- Earnings per Share (EPS) is a financial metric that indicates the profitability of a company on a per-share basis. It is one of the most important metrics for assessing a company's performance and is often used by investors to gauge a company's profitability and make investment decisions.

($)Book value:- Book value refers to the net asset value of a company, calculated by subtracting its total liabilities from its total assets. It represents the theoretical value of a company's assets that would be left over for shareholders if all liabilities were paid off.

($)Face value:- Face value, also known as par value or nominal value, refers to the value of a security or financial instrument as stated on the instrument itself. For stocks, face value is typically a nominal amount assigned when the stock is issued and has no relation to the market price of the stock.

($)Shareholding pattern:- Shareholding pattern refers to the distribution of shares among various categories of shareholders in a company. It provides insights into the ownership structure of the company, including the percentage of shares held by promoters, institutional investors, retail investors, and other categories.

Understanding the shareholding pattern is important for investors, analysts, and regulatory authorities to assess the level of ownership concentration, influence of key stakeholders, and potential impact on corporate governance.

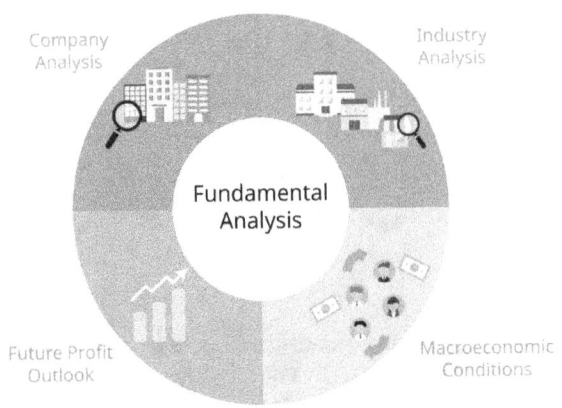

Market Cap

Market capitalization, often referred to as market cap, is a measure of a company's total value as determined by the stock market. It is calculated by multiplying the current share price by the total number of outstanding shares. Market cap helps investors understand the relative size of a company compared to others in the market and categorize companies into different tiers.

Calculation of Market Capitalization:

$Market\ Capitalization = Share\ Price \times Number\ of\ Outstanding\ Shares$

Categories of Market Capitalization:

Large-Cap:

Definition: Companies with a market cap of Rs 20,000 Crores or more.

Characteristics: Established companies with a stable performance record, often market leaders in their industry.

Example: Reliance Industries, TCS, Infosys.

Mid-Cap:

Definition: Companies with a market cap between Rs 5000 to Rs20,000 Crores.

Characteristics: Companies that are typically in growth phases and may offer more growth potential but come with higher risk compared to large-cap stocks.

Example: Apollo Hospitals, Adani Enterprises.

Small-Cap:
Definition: Companies with a market cap 5000 crores or less.
Characteristics: Younger companies with significant growth potential but higher volatility and risk.
Example: Deepak Nitrite, JK Paper.

Importance of Market Capitalization

-Investment Decisions:

Risk Assessment: Market cap helps investors assess the risk associated with investing in a company. Generally, larger companies are considered safer investments due to their established market position and financial stability.
Growth Potential: Smaller companies may offer higher growth potential but come with increased volatility and risk.

-Portfolio Diversification:
Investors often diversify their portfolios by including a mix of large-cap, mid-cap, and small-cap stocks to balance risk and potential returns.

-Index Inclusion:
Market cap determines a company's inclusion in stock market indices like the Nifty 50 or SENSEX. Being part of these indices can increase a company's visibility and attract more investors.

-Valuation Metric:
Market cap provides a quick valuation metric that can be used to compare companies within the same industry.

-Mergers and Acquisitions:
Companies looking to acquire others often consider market cap to evaluate the size and valuation of potential targets.

P/E Ratio

The Price-to-Earnings (P/E) ratio is a commonly used metric in fundamental analysis to assess a company's valuation relative to its earnings. It indicates how much investors are willing to pay for each dollar of earnings. The P/E ratio is calculated by dividing the current market price of a stock by its earnings per share (EPS).

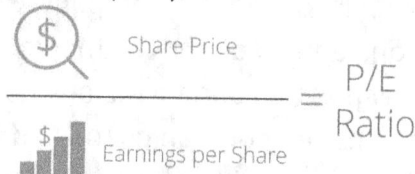

$$\frac{\text{Share Price}}{\text{Earnings per Share}} = \text{P/E Ratio}$$

Interpretation of the P/E Ratio:
High P/E Ratio: Indicates that investors expect high growth rates in the future.
May suggest that the stock is overvalued if the growth expectations are not met.

Low P/E Ratio: Indicates that the stock may be undervalued or that the company is experiencing difficulties.
May also suggest a stable, mature company with modest growth prospects.

Factors Influencing the P/E Ratio:

Earnings Growth: Companies with high growth rates typically have higher P/E ratios.

Industry Norms: Different industries have different average P/E ratios. Comparing a company's P/E ratio with its industry average provides context.

Market Conditions: Bullish markets often see higher P/E ratios, while bearish markets may see lower P/E ratios.

Company Risk: Companies perceived as higher risk may have lower P/E ratios, reflecting the risk premium required by investors.

Investor Sentiment: Positive investor sentiment and confidence in a company's future can drive up the P/E ratio.

P/E Ratio in Investment Decisions:

Comparative Valuation: Comparing the P/E ratios of companies within the same industry helps identify potentially undervalued or overvalued stocks.

Growth vs. Value Investing: Growth investors may favor companies with higher P/E ratios, expecting continued earnings growth.
Value investors look for lower P/E ratios, aiming to find undervalued companies with strong fundamentals.

Historical Comparison: Comparing a company's current P/E ratio to its historical P/E ratios can provide insights into how the market currently values the company's earnings relative to the past.

A lower P/E may mean the company is undervalued (a potentially good buy), while a higher P/E might indicate overvaluation (potentially overpriced).

Limitations of the P/E Ratio:

Earnings Volatility: Companies with volatile earnings can have misleading P/E ratios.

Different Accounting Practices: Variations in accounting practices can affect reported earnings and thus the P/E ratio.

No Insight into Future Growth: The P/E ratio alone does not provide insights into future earnings growth or the reasons behind the earnings.

Non-Applicability to Non-Earning Companies: Companies with negative earnings or no earnings cannot be evaluated using the P/E ratio.

P/B Ratio

The Price-to-Book (P/B) ratio is a financial metric used to compare a company's market value to its book value. It is calculated by dividing the current market price per share by the book value per share (BVPS). This ratio helps investors assess whether a stock is undervalued or overvalued by comparing the market's valuation of a company to its actual net asset value.

Calculation of P/B Ratio:

$$\text{Price to Book Ratio (P/B)} = \frac{\text{Market Capitalization}}{\text{Book Value of Equity (BVE)}}$$

Interpretation of the P/B Ratio:

P/B Ratio < 1: Indicates that the stock may be undervalued. Suggests that the market price is less than the company's book value, potentially a good buying opportunity.

P/B Ratio = 1: Indicates that the market price is equal to the book value.
Suggests the stock is fairly valued.

P/B Ratio > 1: Indicates that the stock may be overvalued. Suggests that the market price is greater than the company's book value, which could imply that investors expect high future growth.

Factors Influencing the P/B Ratio:

Industry Norms: Different industries have different average P/B ratios. Capital-intensive industries like manufacturing often have lower P/B ratios, while service and technology industries may have higher P/B ratios.

Company's Asset Base: Companies with significant tangible assets typically have lower P/B ratios. Those with intangible assets like intellectual property may have higher P/B ratios.

Return on Equity (ROE): Companies with high ROE tend to have higher P/B ratios as investors expect higher returns on equity.

Growth Prospects: High growth prospects can lead to higher P/B ratios, reflecting investor optimism about future earnings and asset value growth.

Market Sentiment: Positive sentiment and investor confidence can drive up the P/B ratio, while negative sentiment can lower it.

P/B Ratio in Investment Decisions:

Value Investing: Value investors look for stocks with low P/B ratios, considering them as potentially undervalued by the market.

Comparative Valuation: Comparing the P/B ratios of companies within the same industry can help identify undervalued or overvalued stocks.

Assessing Financial Health: A low P/B ratio can indicate potential financial distress or undervaluation, while a high P/B ratio may reflect strong financial health or overvaluation.

Examples of P/B Ratio Application:
Low P/B Ratio Example: A manufacturing company with a P/B ratio of 0.8 may indicate that the market is valuing the company at less than its net asset value, suggesting potential undervaluation.

High P/B Ratio Example: A tech company with a P/B ratio of 5 may indicate that the market is valuing the company significantly above its net asset value, suggesting high growth expectations.

Limitations of the P/B Ratio:
Intangible Assets: The P/B ratio may undervalue companies with significant intangible assets like patents and trademarks that are not fully reflected in the book value.

Asset Valuation: The book value is based on historical costs and may not reflect the current market value of assets.

Industry Variations: P/B ratios vary widely across industries, making cross-industry comparisons less meaningful.

Doesn't Reflect Earnings: The P/B ratio doesn't consider the company's earnings or profitability, which can be crucial for investment decisions.

Industry P/E

The Industry P/E (Price-to-Earnings) ratio is a valuation metric that provides an average P/E ratio for all the companies within a particular industry. This ratio helps investors gauge the relative valuation of a company compared to its industry peers. By comparing a company's P/E ratio to the industry average, investors can determine if the company is overvalued, undervalued, or fairly valued relative to other companies in the same sector.

Key Aspects of Industry P/E:

Benchmarking: The industry P/E ratio serves as a benchmark for evaluating the valuation of individual companies within that industry.

Contextual Comparison: Helps in understanding how a company is valued compared to its peers, providing context to its individual P/E ratio.

Investment Decisions: Assists investors in making more informed decisions by identifying potential investment opportunities or risks based on relative valuation.

How to Use Industry P/E Ratio:

Compare Individual P/E to Industry P/E: If a company's P/E ratio is lower than the industry P/E, it may indicate that the company is undervalued relative to its peers.

If a company's P/E ratio is higher than the industry P/E, it may indicate that the company is overvalued relative to its peers.

Assessing Growth Potential:
A higher P/E ratio compared to the industry average may suggest that investors expect higher growth from the company.

A lower P/E ratio may indicate lower growth expectations or potential undervaluation.

Risk Evaluation: Understanding how a company is valued relative to its industry can help assess the risk associated with the investment. Overvalued companies might be more susceptible to price corrections.

Examples:
Technology Industry:
Industry P/E Ratio: 25
Company A P/E Ratio: 30
Interpretation: Company A is valued higher than the industry average, possibly due to higher growth expectations or market optimism.

Company B P/E Ratio: 20
Interpretation: Company B is valued lower than the industry average, suggesting it might be undervalued or facing challenges not shared by its peers.

Healthcare Industry:
Industry P/E Ratio: 18

Company C P/E Ratio: 15
Interpretation: Company C might be undervalued or operating under specific risks or market conditions that are affecting its valuation.

Company D P/E Ratio: 22
Interpretation: Company D is valued higher than the industry average, possibly due to strong growth prospects or a robust market position.

Factors Affecting Industry P/E Ratio:

Growth Prospects: Industries with high growth potential, such as technology or biotech, often have higher P/E ratios.

Economic Conditions: Cyclical industries like automotive or construction may see fluctuations in their industry P/E ratios based on economic cycles.

Risk and Stability: Stable industries like utilities or consumer staples often have lower P/E ratios due to steady earnings and lower risk.

Market Sentiment: Investor sentiment towards an industry can significantly impact its P/E ratio. Positive outlooks can drive up P/E ratios, while negative sentiment can depress them.

Limitations of Industry P/E Ratio:

Varied Company Sizes: The industry P/E ratio may not account for the size differences among companies, which can affect their valuations.

Different Business Models: Companies within the same industry can have different business models, affecting their profitability and growth prospects, and thus their P/E ratios.

Market Conditions: Short-term market conditions and sentiment can affect P/E ratios, leading to temporary misvaluations.

Lack of Uniform Accounting Practices: Differences in accounting practices among companies can affect reported earnings, thereby impacting P/E ratios.

Debt-to-Equity (D/E) ratio

The Debt-to-Equity (D/E) ratio is a financial metric used to evaluate a company's financial leverage by comparing its total liabilities to its shareholder equity. This ratio provides insight into the extent to which a company is financing its operations through debt versus wholly-owned funds.

$$\text{Debt to Equity Ratio (D/E)} = \frac{\text{Total Debt}}{\text{Total Shareholders Equity}}$$

Components of the D/E Ratio:

Total Liabilities: This includes both short-term and long-term liabilities such as loans, bonds, accounts payable, and other obligations.

Shareholder Equity: This represents the net assets owned by shareholders and is calculated as total assets minus total liabilities. It includes common stock, retained earnings, and additional paid-in capital.

Interpretation of the D/E Ratio:

High D/E Ratio: Indicates a company is heavily financed by debt.
Suggests higher financial risk due to the obligation to service debt (interest payments and principal repayment).

Companies with high D/E ratios might be more susceptible to economic downturns and higher interest rates.

Low D/E Ratio: Indicates a company is primarily financed by shareholder equity.
Suggests lower financial risk and potentially more stable earnings.

Companies with low D/E ratios might have more conservative financial practices and less burden from debt.

Industry Variations:

Capital-Intensive Industries: Industries like utilities, telecommunications, and manufacturing often have higher D/E ratios due to the need for significant capital investment.

Service and Technology Industries:
These industries might have lower D/E ratios as they often require less capital investment.

Uses of the D/E Ratio:

Assessing Financial Risk: Investors and creditors use the D/E ratio to evaluate a company's financial risk. A high ratio might deter investment due to the higher financial risk associated with high debt levels.

Comparative Analysis: Comparing the D/E ratio of a company to its industry peers provides insight into its financial leverage relative to others in the same sector.

Evaluating Financial Health: A balanced D/E ratio indicates sound financial health and prudent financial management.

Examples of D/E Ratio Application:
Company A (Tech Industry):
Total Liabilities: $500 million
Shareholder Equity: $1 billion
D/E Ratio: 0.5

Interpretation: The company is conservatively financed with more reliance on equity than debt, indicating lower financial risk.

Company B (Manufacturing Industry):
Total Liabilities: $1.5 billion
Shareholder Equity: $1 billion
D/E Ratio: 1.5

Interpretation: The company has higher financial leverage, indicating greater financial risk but potentially higher returns due to the use of debt for growth and expansion.

Limitations of the D/E Ratio:
Variations in Accounting Practices: Differences in how companies report liabilities and equity can affect the comparability of D/E ratios.

Exclusion of Off-Balance Sheet Liabilities: Some liabilities might not appear on the balance sheet, affecting the accuracy of the D/E ratio.

Industry Differences: Industry norms for the D/E ratio vary, making cross-industry comparisons less meaningful.

Return on Equity (ROE)

Return on Equity (ROE) is a financial ratio that measures a company's ability to generate profits from its shareholders' equity. It indicates how efficiently a company is using the money invested by its shareholders to generate earnings.

$$\text{Return on Equity (ROE)} = \frac{\text{Net Income}}{\text{Average Total Equity}}$$

ROE is a key metric for assessing the profitability and financial performance of a company.

Components of ROE:

Net Income: The total profit of the company after all expenses, taxes, and interest have been deducted from total revenue. It is typically found at the bottom of the income statement.

Shareholder Equity: The residual interest in the assets of the company after deducting liabilities. It includes common stock, retained earnings, and additional paid-in capital, and is found on the balance sheet.

Interpretation of ROE:

High ROE: Indicates that the company is effectively generating profits from its equity base.
Suggests strong financial performance and efficient use of shareholders' investments.
A high ROE can be attractive to investors as it implies good returns on their investments.

Low ROE: Indicates that the company may not be efficiently utilizing its equity base to generate profits.
Could suggest poor financial performance or inefficient management.

Uses of ROE:

Investment Decisions: Investors use ROE to compare the profitability of companies within the same industry. A higher ROE typically indicates a more profitable and potentially better-managed company.

Performance Measurement: ROE is a key metric for assessing management's effectiveness in generating profits from shareholders' investments.

Benchmarking: Companies compare their ROE with industry averages to evaluate their performance relative to peers.

Factors Affecting ROE:

Profit Margins: Higher profit margins can lead to a higher ROE as the company retains more profit from its revenues.

Asset Turnover: Efficient use of assets to generate sales can improve ROE by increasing net income relative to equity.

Financial Leverage: The use of debt can amplify ROE, as long as the returns generated from the borrowed funds exceed the cost of debt.

Examples of ROE Application:
Company A (Retail Industry):
Net Income: $200 million
Shareholder Equity: $1 billion
ROE: 20%
Interpretation: Company A is generating 20 cents of profit for every dollar of equity, indicating strong financial performance.

Company B (Technology Industry):
Net Income: $50 million
Shareholder Equity: $500 million
ROE: 10%
Interpretation: Company B is generating 10 cents of profit for every dollar of equity, indicating moderate financial performance.

Limitations of ROE:

Debt Influence: High levels of debt can inflate ROE, making a company appear more profitable than it actually is due to increased financial risk.

Asset Revaluation: Changes in the valuation of assets can affect shareholder equity and thus ROE, potentially distorting the true profitability.

Industry Variations: ROE varies across industries, so comparisons should be made within the same industry to be meaningful.

Earnings per Share (EPS)

Earnings per Share (EPS) is a financial metric that indicates the profitability of a company on a per-share basis. It is one of the most important metrics for assessing a company's performance and is often used by investors to gauge a company's profitability and make investment decisions.

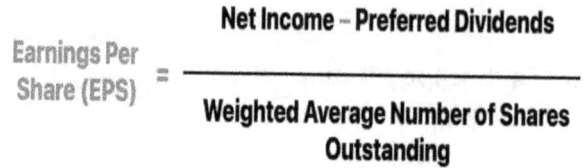

$$\text{Earnings Per Share (EPS)} = \frac{\text{Net Income} - \text{Preferred Dividends}}{\text{Weighted Average Number of Shares Outstanding}}$$

Components of EPS:

Net Income: The total profit of the company after all expenses, taxes, and interest have been deducted from total revenue. This is typically found at the bottom of the income statement.

Preferred Dividends: Dividends that are paid to preferred shareholders. These are subtracted from net income because EPS is meant to represent the income available to common shareholders.

Weighted Average Number of Outstanding Shares: The number of shares outstanding during the reporting period, weighted by the time they were outstanding. This accounts for any changes in the number of shares due to stock splits, share buybacks, or new issuance of shares during the period.

Interpretation of EPS:

High EPS: Indicates that the company is generating significant profit for each share of common stock, which is typically seen as a positive sign of financial health.

Low EPS: Indicates lower profitability on a per-share basis, which might be a concern for investors, especially if the EPS is declining over time.

Growth in EPS: Consistent growth in EPS over time is often viewed positively by investors as it suggests that the company is effectively increasing its profitability.

Uses of EPS:

Investment Decisions: Investors use EPS to assess a company's profitability and make comparisons with other companies in the same industry.
A higher EPS can indicate a potentially more profitable and valuable investment.

Valuation Metrics: EPS is a critical component of various valuation metrics, such as the Price-to-Earnings (P/E) ratio, which helps investors determine if a stock is overvalued or undervalued.

Performance Benchmarking: Companies use EPS to benchmark their financial performance against competitors and industry standards.

Examples of EPS Calculation:
Company A:
Net Income: $100 million
Preferred Dividends: $10 million
Weighted Average Shares Outstanding: 50 million

- Basic EPS:

$$\frac{100 \text{ million} - 10 \text{ million}}{50 \text{ million}} = 1.8$$

Company B:
Net Income: $150 million
Preferred Dividends: $5 million
Weighted Average Shares Outstanding: 75 million
- Basic EPS:

$$\frac{150 \text{ million} - 5 \text{ million}}{75 \text{ million}} = 1.93$$

Limitations of EPS:
Not Adjusted for Growth: EPS does not account for the growth potential of the company or the sustainability of current earnings levels.

Accounting Differences: Differences in accounting practices can affect the comparability of EPS between companies.

Exclusion of Non-Recurring Items: EPS can be influenced by non-recurring items like asset sales or restructuring charges, which might not reflect the core operating performance of the company.

Share Dilution: Basic EPS does not consider the potential dilution from convertible securities, which can overstate the actual earnings per share available to common shareholders.

Book value

Book value refers to the net asset value of a company, calculated by subtracting its total liabilities from its total assets. It represents the theoretical value of a company's assets that would be left over for shareholders if all liabilities were paid off.

Calculation of Book Value:

Book Value=Total Assets-Total Liabilities

Components of Book Value:
Total Assets: Includes all assets owned by the company, such as cash, inventory, property, plant, equipment, and investments.

Total Liabilities: Includes all debts and obligations of the company, such as loans, accounts payable, accrued expenses, and long-term liabilities.

Significance of Book Value:

Shareholder Equity: Book value is directly related to shareholder equity, as it represents the portion of assets owned by shareholders after deducting liabilities.

Financial Health: Book value is used to assess a company's financial health and solvency. A higher book value generally indicates a stronger financial position.

Valuation Metric: Book value per share is a key metric used by investors to evaluate a company's stock price relative to its book value. It is calculated by dividing the book value by the number of outstanding shares.

Book Value vs. Market Value:

Book Value: Represents the accounting value of a company's assets and liabilities.
Generally historical and does not reflect current market conditions or investor sentiment.

Market Value: Represents the current market price of a company's stock, determined by supply and demand in the stock market.
Can be higher or lower than book value, influenced by factors such as growth prospects, industry trends, and investor perceptions.

Uses of Book Value:

Valuation Analysis: Investors use book value per share as a valuation metric to assess whether a stock is undervalued or overvalued relative to its book value.

Comparative Analysis: Book value is used to compare the financial strength and asset base of companies within the same industry or sector.

Investment Decisions: Book value provides insights into a company's asset composition, debt levels, and overall financial stability, helping investors make informed investment decisions.

Limitations of Book Value:

Market Conditions: Book value may not accurately reflect a company's true value in rapidly changing market conditions, especially for companies with significant intangible assets or market-driven valuations.

Intangible Assets: Book value does not account for intangible assets such as intellectual property, brand value, or goodwill, which can be significant contributors to a company's overall value.

Inflation and Depreciation: Book value may be affected by inflation and depreciation, leading to potential distortions in asset values over time.

"Use book value as a starting point to try and establish the value of the enterprise."

– Walter Schloss

Book Value

The sum of the amounts of all the line items in the shareholders' equity section on a company's balance sheet.

Face value

Face value, also known as par value or nominal value, refers to the value of a security or financial instrument as stated on the instrument itself. For stocks, face value is typically a nominal amount assigned when the stock is issued and has no relation to the market price of the stock.

Key Points about Face Value:

Nominal Amount: Face value is a nominal amount assigned to a security at the time of issuance. It is often a small value, such as Rs1, Rs10, or Rs100, and does not reflect the market value or intrinsic value of the security.

Legal and Accounting Purposes: Face value is used for legal and accounting purposes to determine the initial value of a security and to calculate certain financial metrics.

Fixed vs. Variable Face Value:

For **fixed-income** securities like bonds, face value represents the amount that the issuer promises to repay to the bondholder at maturity. It is also used to calculate interest payments.

For stocks, face value is typically a nominal amount and does not affect the market price or value of the stock. In many cases, stocks have a very low or symbolic face value, such as Rs0.01 per share.

No Relation to Market Price: The face value of a stock or bond does not reflect its market price. Market price is determined by supply and demand in the market and can be higher or lower than the face value.

Examples of Face Value:

Stocks: A company may issue common shares with a face value of $0.01 per share. However, the market price of these shares can fluctuate significantly based on factors such as company performance, industry trends, and investor sentiment.

Bonds: A corporate bond may have a face value of Rs1,000, representing the amount that the issuer will repay to the bondholder at maturity. The bond's market price may be higher or lower than the face value depending on interest rates and other market factors.

Importance of Face Value:

Legal Obligation: For bonds and other debt securities, face value represents the legal obligation of the issuer to repay the principal amount to the investor at maturity.

Calculation of Metrics: Face value is used in various financial calculations, such as calculating interest payments for bonds and determining the book value of shares for accounting purposes.

Historical Significance: While face value may not have a direct impact on market pricing, it has historical significance and is used in financial reporting and regulatory filings.

Face Value vs. Market Value:

Face Value:
- Nominal value stated on the security itself.
- Used for legal, accounting, and contractual purposes.
- Fixed for bonds, nominal for stocks.

Market Value:
-Current price at which the security is traded in the market.
-Determined by supply and demand, company performance, economic conditions, and other factors.
-Can be higher or lower than face value.

"Courage taught me no matter how bad a crisis gets ... any sound investment will eventually pay off."
– Carlos Slim Helu

Shareholding pattern

Shareholding pattern refers to the distribution of shares among various categories of shareholders in a company. It provides insights into the ownership structure of the company, including the percentage of shares held by promoters, institutional investors, retail investors, and other categories. Understanding the shareholding pattern is important for investors, analysts, and regulatory authorities to assess the level of ownership concentration, influence of key stakeholders, and potential impact on corporate governance.

Components of Shareholding Pattern:

Promoters or Promoter Group:

Promoters are individuals or entities who founded the company or played a significant role in its establishment. They typically hold a substantial stake and may include founders, management, and their relatives.

Promoter holding is often categorized into promoter group, individual promoters, and their pledged shares (if any).

Institutional Investors:

Institutional investors include mutual funds, insurance companies, pension funds, banks, foreign institutional investors (FIIs), and other institutional entities that invest in the company's shares.

Institutional holding indicates the level of interest and confidence institutional investors have in the company.

Public Shareholding:

Public shareholding refers to shares held by individual investors, retail investors, non-institutional investors, and any other entities that are not part of the promoter group or institutional investors.

It includes shares held by retail investors through direct investment or through mutual funds, as well as shares held by high net worth individuals (HNIs) and other non-institutional entities.

Government Holding:
In the case of government-owned companies or companies with government participation, government holding represents the shares held by government entities or agencies.

Non-Promoter and Non-Institutional Holding:
This category includes shares held by individuals, trusts, corporate bodies, and any other entities that do not fall under the promoter or institutional categories.

Importance of Shareholding Pattern:
Ownership Structure:
Shareholding pattern reveals the ownership structure of the company, including the level of control exercised by promoters, institutional investors, and public shareholders.

Corporate Governance:
It provides insights into corporate governance practices, transparency, and the extent of influence key stakeholders have on decision-making processes.

Investor Confidence:
A balanced and diversified shareholding pattern, with significant institutional and public participation, can enhance investor confidence and improve market liquidity.

Regulatory Compliance:
Companies are required to disclose their shareholding pattern regularly as per regulatory requirements. This information helps regulators monitor ownership changes and ensure compliance with relevant laws and regulations.

Investment Decisions:
Investors and analysts use shareholding pattern data to assess the stability of ownership, potential risks related to concentration of shares, and to make informed investment decisions.

Shareholding Pattern Reporting:

Quarterly Disclosure:
Listed companies are required to disclose their shareholding pattern on a quarterly basis as part of their financial reporting obligations.

Annual Reports:
Shareholding pattern is also included in the annual reports of companies, providing a comprehensive view of ownership trends over time.

Stock Exchange Filings:
Companies may also disclose changes in shareholding pattern through filings with stock exchanges as per regulatory requirements.

Key Ratios Derived from Shareholding Pattern:

Promoter Holding Percentage:
Calculated as the percentage of shares held by promoters and promoter group relative to total shares outstanding.

- Formula:

$$\text{Promoter Holding Percentage} = \frac{\text{Promoter Holding}}{\text{Total Shares Outstanding}} \times 100$$

Institutional Holding Percentage:
Represents the percentage of shares held by institutional investors relative to total shares outstanding.

- Formula:

$$\text{Institutional Holding Percentage} = \frac{\text{Institutional Holding}}{\text{Total Shares Outstanding}} \times 100$$

Public Shareholding Percentage:
Indicates the percentage of shares held by public shareholders (excluding promoters and institutional investors) relative to total shares outstanding.

- Formula:

$$\text{Public Shareholding Percentage} = \frac{\text{Public Shareholding}}{\text{Total Shares Outstanding}} \times 10$$

Shareholding Pattern

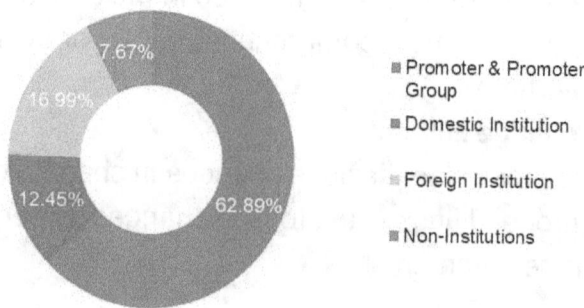

Denary Golden Guidelines

Stock selection criteria

- 👉 CURRENT QUARTERLY EARNINGS - 25% ↑ (more than)
- 👉 ROE - 17% ↑ (more than)
- 👉 CAGR - 25% ↑ (more than)
- 👉 SUPPLY AND DEMAND - (outstanding share)
- 👉 FII & DII & MUTUAL FUND - (Increasing shareholding value)
- 👉 INVEST IN LARGE CAP - (QUALITY STOCKS)
- 👉 NEW IN COMPANY - (SOMETHING NEW IN COMPANY)
- 👉 LIABILITIES TO ASSETS RATIO - (1:2 RATIO)
- 👉 PE LESS THAN 20 - (COSIDERED AS UNDERVALUED)
- 👉 OVERALL MARKET TREND - (UP TREND)

There is 94% chance that ur stock, selected on above criteria will make you profit.

On Above criteria:-

Sl.no	Stock Name	Sep-22	Sep-23	Mar-24
	LARGE CAPITAL			
1	Divis's Lab	3600	3700	3600
2	SBI Cards	915	839	707
3	Varun Beverages	540	909	1423
4	IRCTC	711	725	937
	MID CAPITAL			
5	Jindal steel &power	430	698	839
6	Tata Communication	1357	1249	2011
7	Coromandal Int	1043	1124	1114
8	Motherson Sumi	65	66	67
9	Crisil	3203	3897	4927
10	oil india	193	281	630
11	Fine org IND	6523	4984	4233
	SMALL CAPITAL			
12	G K Infraprojects	1345	1269	1221
13	Deepak Fertilizers	885	605	507
14	Easy trip planners	48	41	48
15	Brightcom Group	41	16	17
16	ASM Technologies	580	479	978
17	BLS Int	128	288	382
18	Lancer Containers	41	85	90
19	Aditya Vision LTD	1478	2435	3525
20	ESAB India	3240	5450	5075

Gambling vs. Trading

1. Definition:

Gambling: Involves placing bets on uncertain outcomes with the primary intent of winning money. This can include activities like casino games, sports betting, and lotteries.

Trading: Involves buying and selling financial instruments such as stocks, bonds, commodities, or currencies with the aim of making a profit. Trading is based on market analysis, trends, and economic indicators.

2. Basis of Decisions:

Gambling: Decisions are often based on chance, luck, or hunches. The outcome is usually unpredictable and relies heavily on probability.

Trading: Decisions are typically based on research, analysis, and strategy. Traders use technical analysis, fundamental analysis, and market news to make informed decisions.

3. Risk and Reward:

Gambling: The risk is usually high, and the odds are often stacked against the player. The potential for loss is significant, and winnings can be sporadic and unpredictable.

Trading: While trading also involves risk, it can be managed through strategies such as diversification, stop-loss orders, and risk management techniques. Successful traders aim for consistent, long-term gains rather than quick wins.

4. Time Horizon:

Gambling: The time horizon is generally short, with outcomes known within minutes or hours.

Trading: The time horizon can vary from short-term (day trading) to long-term (investing). Traders and investors may hold positions for days, weeks, months, or even years.

5. Skill and Knowledge:

Gambling: While some skill may be involved (e.g., poker), most gambling activities rely on chance. Success is often fleeting and inconsistent.

Trading: Success in trading requires skill, knowledge, and experience. Traders must understand market mechanics, financial statements, economic indicators, and trading strategies.

6. Purpose:

Gambling: The primary purpose is entertainment and the thrill of potentially winning money.

Trading: The primary purpose is to grow wealth over time through informed financial decisions.

7. Regulatory Environment:

Gambling: Is heavily regulated, with specific laws and regulations governing casinos, online betting, and lotteries to ensure fairness and prevent fraud.

Trading: Financial markets are also highly regulated to ensure transparency, protect investors, and maintain market integrity. Regulatory bodies oversee trading activities, enforce rules, and monitor for illegal activities such as insider trading.

Trading vs. Investing
1. Time Horizon:
Trading: Involves buying and selling financial instruments with the intention of making quick profits. The time horizon is usually short, ranging from seconds to a few months.

Investing: Involves purchasing assets to hold them for an extended period, typically years or even decades, to achieve long-term financial goals.

2. Approach and Strategy:

Trading: Traders actively seek to profit from short-term market fluctuations. They use technical analysis, charts, and market trends to make decisions. Strategies include day trading, swing trading, and scalping.

Investing: Investors focus on the long-term potential of an asset. They use fundamental analysis to evaluate a company's financial health, management, competitive advantages, and market position. Strategies include value investing, growth investing, and income investing.

3. Frequency of Transactions:

Trading: Involves frequent buying and selling. Traders may execute multiple transactions in a single day.
Investing: Involves fewer transactions. Investors buy and hold assets, making adjustments to their portfolios as needed based on their long-term strategy.

4. Risk and Reward:

Trading: Can offer high rewards but also comes with higher risk. The volatility of short-term market movements can lead to significant gains or losses.

Investing: Generally considered less risky over the long term. The focus on long-term growth helps to ride out market volatility and benefit from compounding returns.

5. Skills and Knowledge:

Trading: Requires a deep understanding of market patterns, technical indicators, and trading platforms. Traders need to be able to react quickly to market changes.

Investing: Requires knowledge of financial statements, company performance, and economic conditions. Investors need to be patient and have the discipline to stick to their long-term plan.

6. Emotional Control:

Trading: Requires a high level of emotional control and discipline. Traders need to avoid making impulsive decisions based on fear or greed.

Investing: Also requires emotional control, but the focus on long-term goals can help investors remain calm during market downturns.

7. Costs and Fees:

Trading: Involves higher transaction costs due to frequent buying and selling. Traders need to consider brokerage fees, commissions, and taxes.

Investing: Generally incurs lower costs over time. Investors may pay initial purchase fees and ongoing management fees for their portfolios but avoid the frequent costs associated with trading.

8. Performance Measurement:

Trading: Success is often measured by short-term gains and the ability to outperform the market over short periods.

Investing: Success is measured by long-term growth and the achievement of financial goals such as retirement, education funding, or wealth accumulation.

TRADING

Trading in the Indian stock market can be approached through various methods and involves different types of instruments. Here's an overview of the key types of trading and the instruments available in the Indian stock market:

Types of Trading:

Intraday Trading:

Description: Buying and selling of stocks on the same day before the market closes.

Objective: Capitalize on short-term price movements.

Risk Level: High due to market volatility within the day.

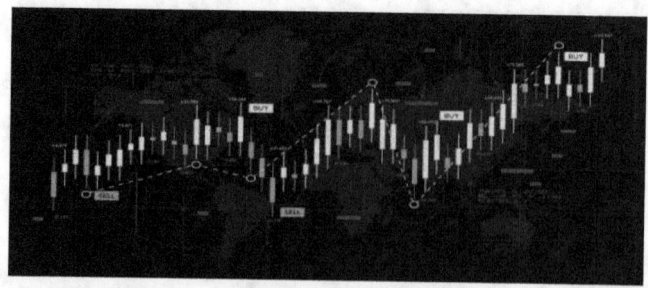

Swing Trading:

Description: Holding stocks for a few days to a few weeks.

Objective: Benefit from 'swings' in stock prices.

Risk Level: Moderate, requires analysis of market trends.

Positional Trading:

Description: Holding stocks for weeks to months.

Objective: Profit from medium to long-term trends.

Risk Level: Lower than intraday or swing trading, but requires patience and analysis.

Long-term Investing:

Description: Holding stocks for several years.

Objective: Achieve growth through appreciation and dividends over a long period.

Risk Level: Lower compared to short-term trading, but involves risk of market downturns.

Scalping:

Description: Executing multiple trades within seconds to minutes to make small profits.

Objective: Accumulate small gains with high-frequency trading.

Risk Level: Very high due to rapid market movements.

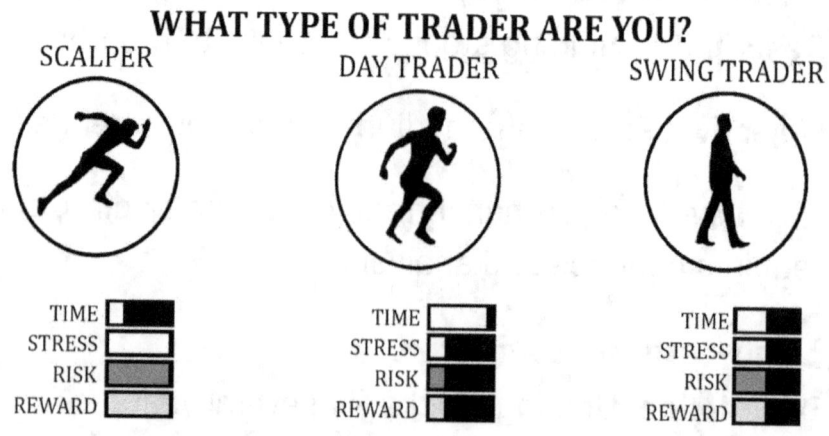

Types of Instruments:

Equities (Stocks):

Description: Shares of ownership in a company.

Trading Platform: NSE (National Stock Exchange), BSE (Bombay Stock Exchange).

Examples: Reliance Industries, TCS, Infosys.

Mutual Funds:

Description: Pooled investment vehicles managed by fund managers.

Types: Equity Funds, Debt Funds, Hybrid Funds, Index Funds.

Examples: HDFC Equity Fund, SBI Bluechip Fund.

Commodities:

Description: Trading of physical goods like gold, silver, crude oil.

Trading Platform: MCX (Multi Commodity Exchange), NCDEX (National Commodity & Derivatives Exchange).

Examples: Gold futures, Crude oil futures.

Derivatives:

Description: Financial instruments deriving their value from underlying assets.

Types: Futures, Options.

Examples: Nifty 50 futures, Reliance call options.

Currencies (Forex):

Description: Trading of currency pairs.

Trading Platform: NSE, BSE.

Examples: USD/INR, EUR/INR.

Trading Platforms:

National Stock Exchange (NSE):
Description: Major stock exchange in India.

Indices: Nifty 50, Nifty Next 50.

Bombay Stock Exchange (BSE):
Description: Asia's first stock exchange.

Indices: Sensex, BSE Midcap.

Multi Commodity Exchange (MCX):
Description: Largest commodity exchange in India.

Commodities: Gold, Silver, Crude Oil.

National Commodity & Derivatives Exchange (NCDEX):
Description: Agricultural commodity exchange.
Commodities: Wheat, Soybean, Cotton.

Technical analysis is a method of evaluating securities by analyzing statistics generated by market activity, such as past prices and volume. Unlike fundamental analysis, which attempts to measure a security's intrinsic value based on business performance, technical analysis focuses on identifying patterns and trends that can predict future price movements.

Price Charts:

Line Charts: Simplest form, showing the closing prices over a specific period.

Bar Charts: Provide more information by displaying the open, high, low, and close (OHLC) prices.

Candlestick Charts: Similar to bar charts but with a more visual representation, showing the price action within a specified period.

Types Of Stock Charts

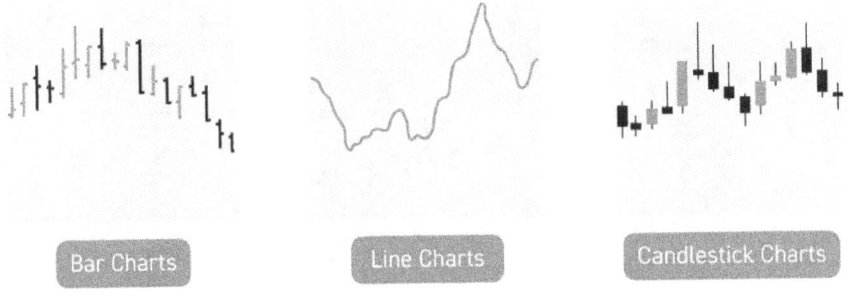

Trends:

Uptrend: A series of higher highs and higher lows, indicating a bullish market.

Downtrend: A series of lower highs and lower lows, indicating a bearish market.

Sideways/Horizontal Trend: When prices move within a range, indicating consolidation.

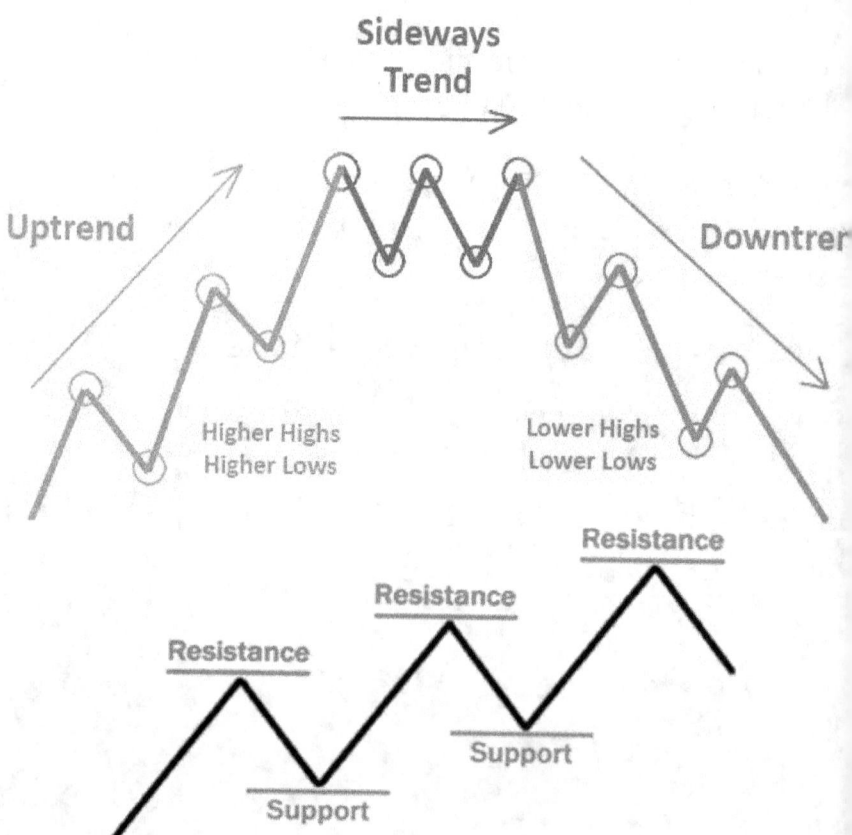

Support and Resistance:

Support: A price level where a downtrend can be expected to pause due to a concentration of buying interest.

Resistance: A price level where an uptrend can be expected to pause due to a concentration of selling interest.

Technical Indicators:

Moving Averages: Smooth out price data to identify the direction of the trend. Common types include Simple Moving Average (SMA) and Exponential Moving Average (EMA).

Relative Strength Index (RSI): Measures the speed and change of price movements, indicating overbought or oversold conditions.

Moving Average Convergence Divergence (MACD): Shows the relationship between two moving averages of a security's price.

Bollinger Bands: Use standard deviation to plot bands above and below a moving average, indicating volatility and potential price reversals.

Stochastic Oscillator: Compares a particular closing price of a security to a range of its prices over a certain period, indicating momentum.

Chart Patterns:

Head and Shoulders: Indicates a potential reversal from an uptrend to a downtrend.

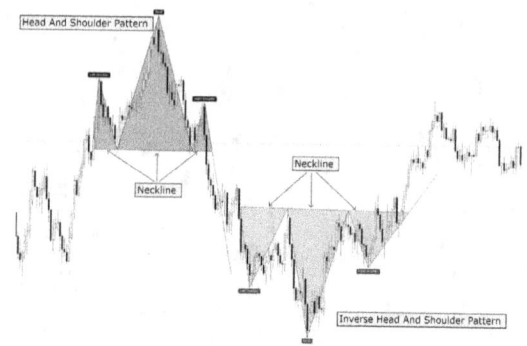

Double Top and Double Bottom: Indicate a potential reversal pattern.

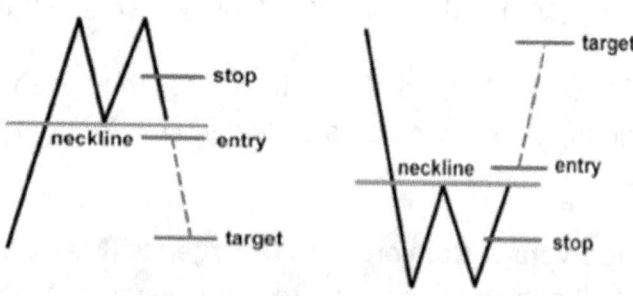

Double Top and Double Bottom

Triangles (Ascending, Descending, Symmetrical): Indicate continuation or reversal, depending on the type and context.

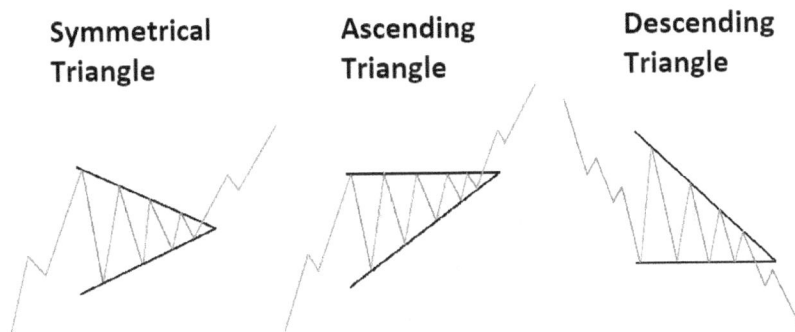

Flags and Pennants: Short-term continuation patterns that indicate a brief consolidation before the previous trend resumes.

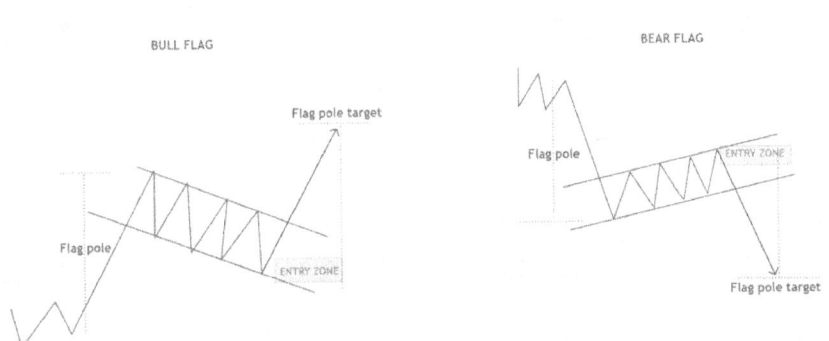

Volume Analysis:

Volume: The number of shares traded in a security. High volume can indicate strong interest and confirm trends.

Volume Oscillators: Indicators like On-Balance Volume (OBV) and Volume Moving Average help assess the strength of a trend.

Steps in Conducting Technical Analysis:

Choose the Right Chart Type: Select a chart type that suits your analysis style and timeframe.

Identify Trends: Determine the prevailing trend and its strength.

Locate Support and Resistance Levels: Identify key price levels where the trend may pause or reverse.

Apply Technical Indicators: Use indicators to confirm trends, measure momentum, and identify potential reversal points.

Analyze Chart Patterns: Look for recognizable patterns that suggest future price movements.

Consider Volume: Analyze volume to confirm price movements and trends.

Make Trading Decisions: Based on your analysis, decide when to enter or exit trades.

Benefits of Technical Analysis:

Timely Insights: Helps traders identify entry and exit points based on market behavior.

Quantitative Analysis: Provides objective criteria for making trading decisions.

Short-Term Trading: Particularly useful for short-term traders looking to capitalize on market volatility.

Trend Identification: Aids in recognizing and following trends, which is crucial for profitable trading.

Limitations of Technical Analysis:

Market Noise: Short-term price movements can be influenced by random market noise.

Lagging Indicators: Many technical indicators are lagging and may not predict future price movements accurately.

Subjectivity: Interpretation of charts and patterns can be subjective and vary between analysts.

Dependence on Past Data: Assumes that past price movements are indicative of future performance, which is not always true.

Basics of technical analysis:

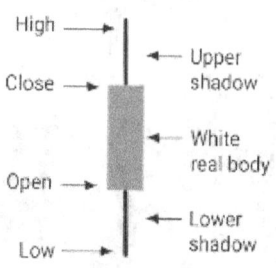
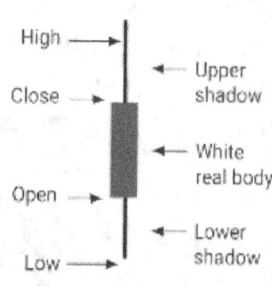
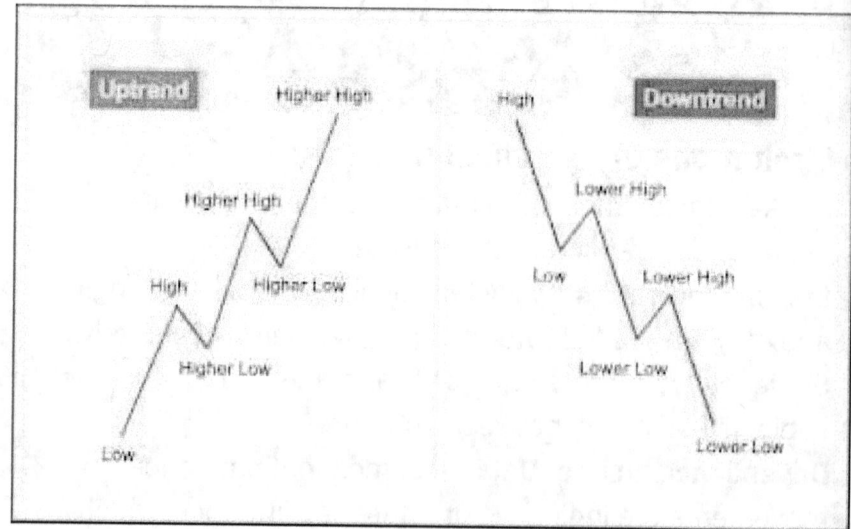

HAMMER

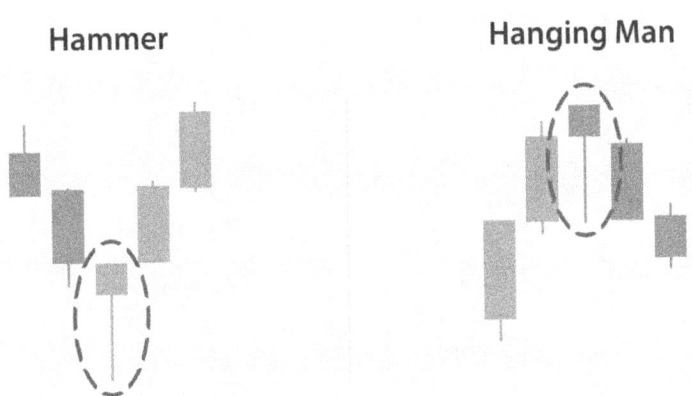

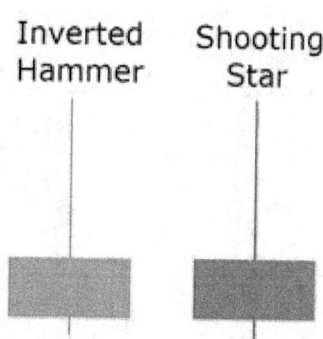

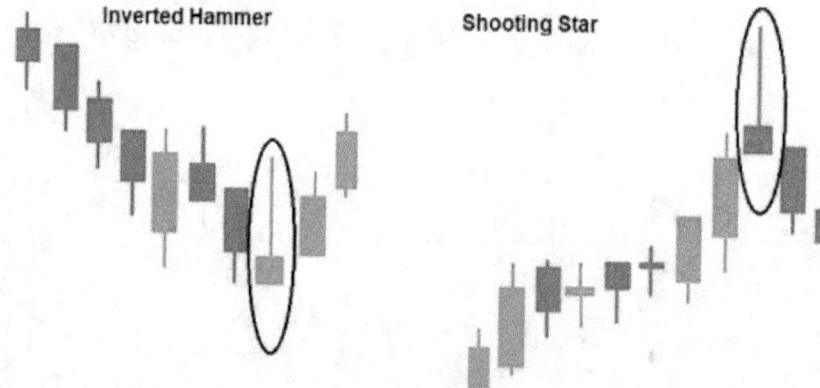

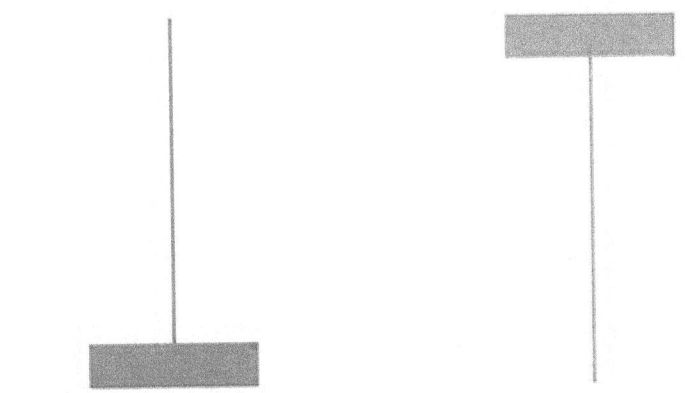

Gravestone Doji   Dragonfly Doji

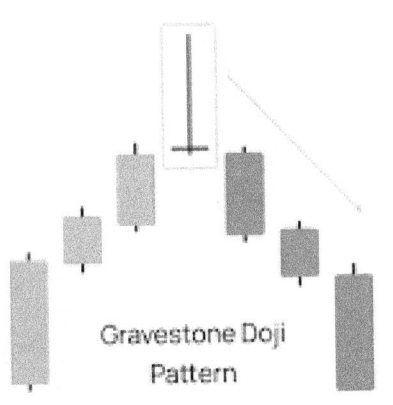

Gravestone Doji Pattern

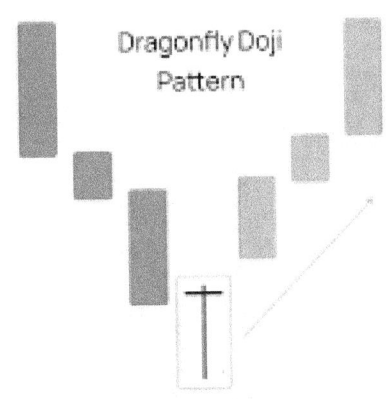

Dragonfly Doji Pattern

Engulfing Patterns

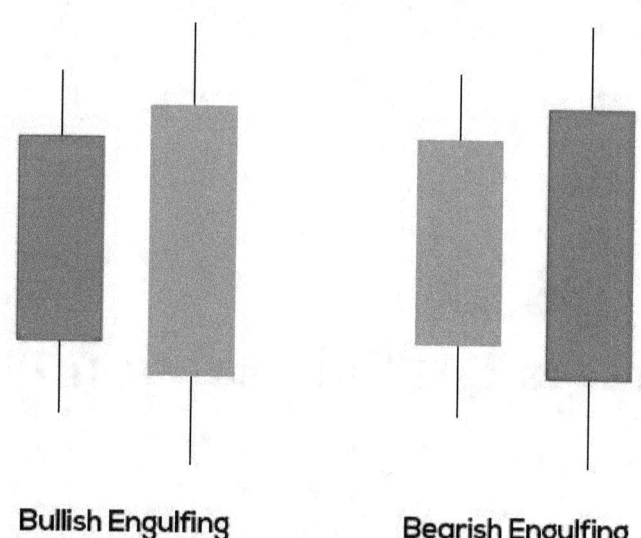

Bullish Engulfing   Bearish Engulfing

BULLISH HARAMI BEARISH HARAMI

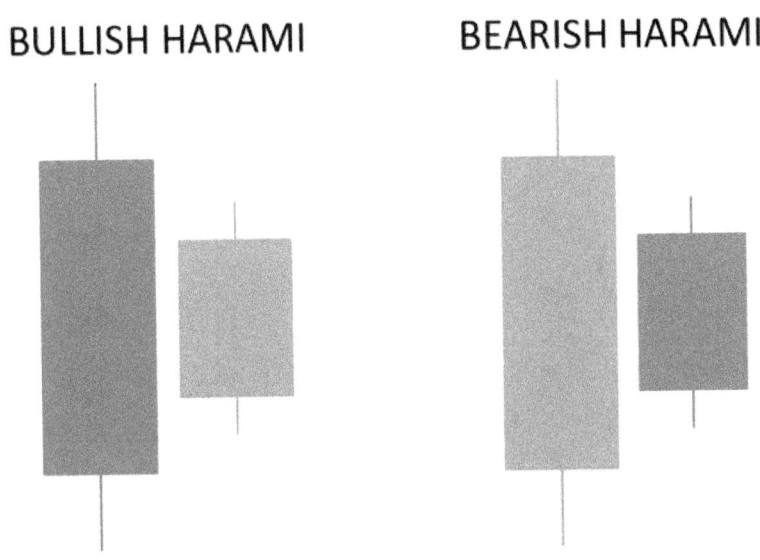

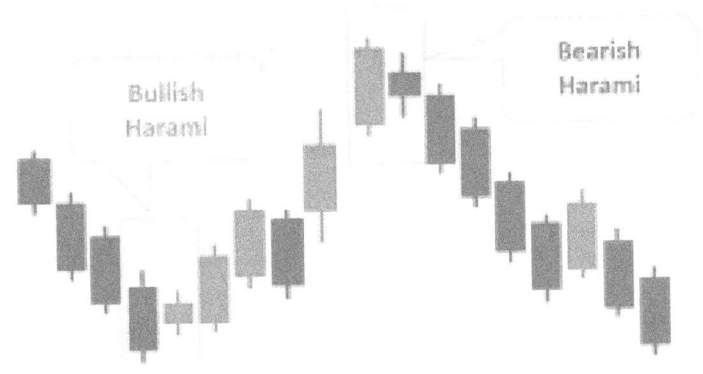

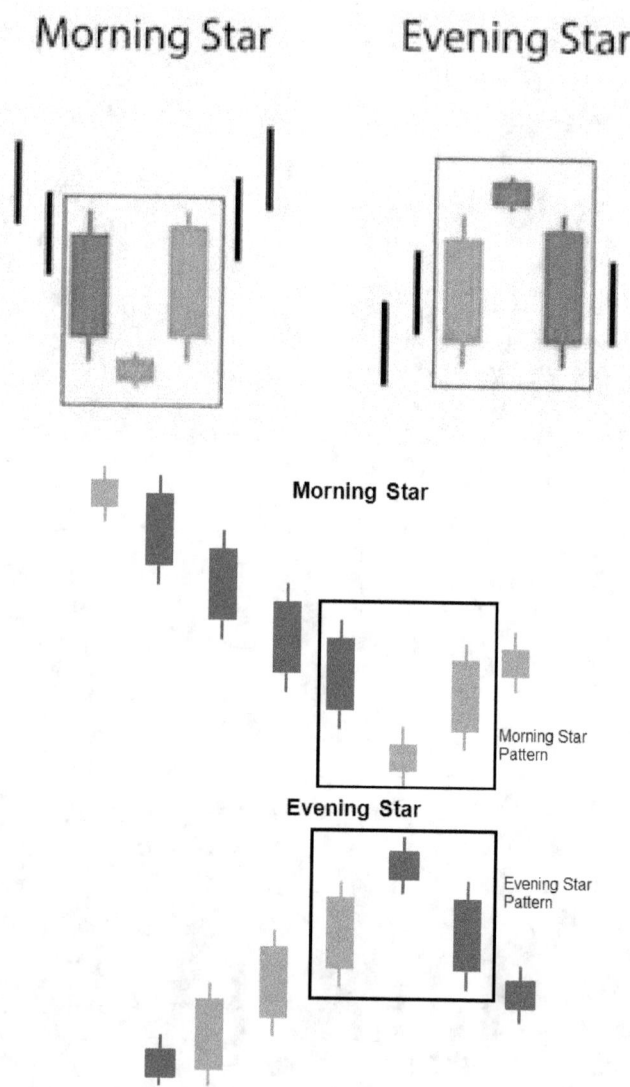

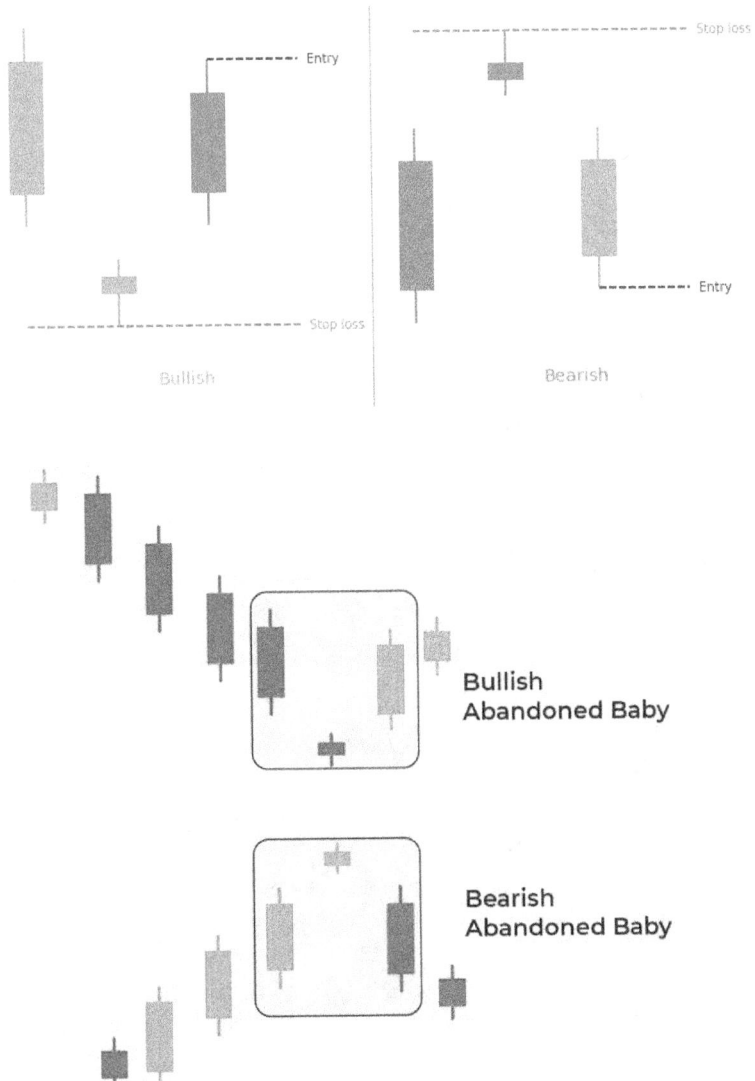

Chart patterns:

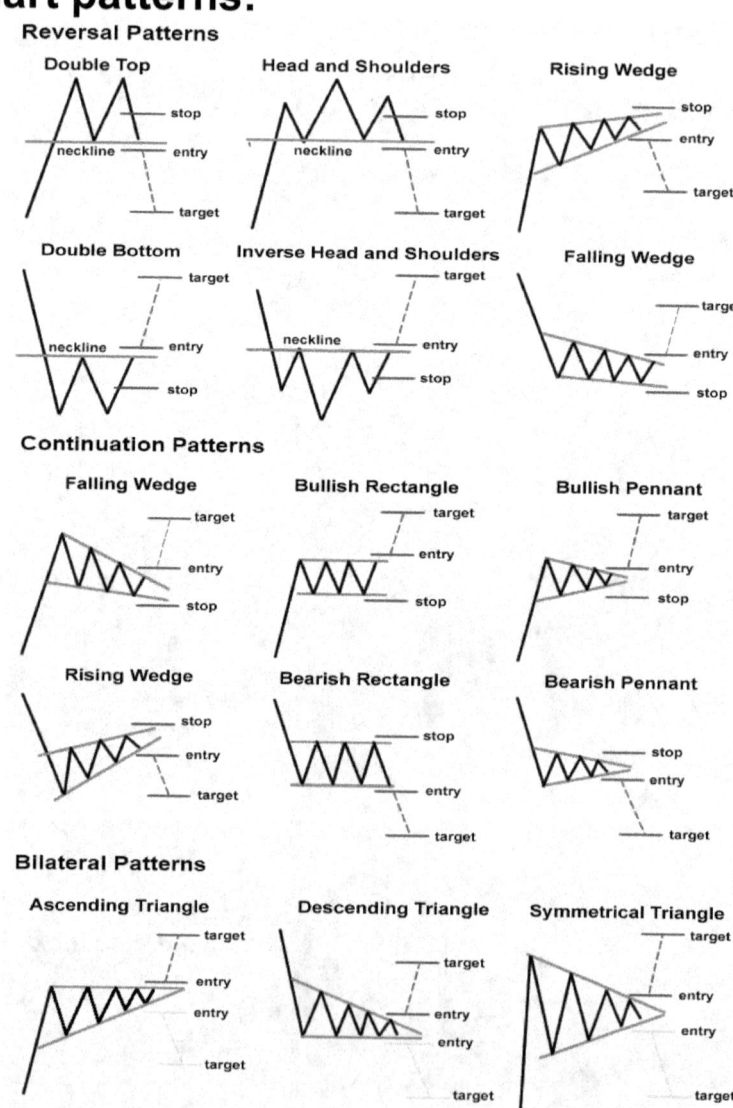

RULES (Discipline)

By adhering to these rules, traders can build a solid foundation for a successful trading journey:
1) Prepare for trade.
2) Limit losses-Define your Stoploss.
3) Do not over trade -1or2 trade per day.
4) Always trade in ur System-Prepare ur strategy.
5) Focus on capital preservation.
6) No Revenge trades.
7) Risk Management.
8) Lock in your profits.
9) Control your Emotions.
10) Avoid TIP trading.

"You will never find fulfillment trading the markets if you don't learn to appreciate and be satisfied with what you already have."— Yvan Byeajee

Things to Do as beginner in Trading :

1)Set Your Trading Goals
Define Objectives: Determine your short-term and long-term trading goals.
Risk-Reward Ratio: Establish how much risk you are willing to take in comparison to the potential reward.

2)Develop a Trading Strategy
Technical Analysis: Use charts, patterns, and technical indicators to identify potential entry and exit points.
Fundamental Analysis: Assess the intrinsic value of the asset and its potential for growth or decline.
Quantitative Analysis: Consider using algorithms and statistical methods to identify trading opportunities.

3)Create a Trading Plan
Entry Criteria: Define the conditions under which you will enter a trade.
Exit Criteria: Set clear criteria for exiting a trade, including profit targets and stop-loss levels.
Position Sizing: Determine the size of your trade based on your risk tolerance and capital.

4) Use Risk Management Techniques

Stop-Loss Orders: Set stop-loss orders to automatically close a trade at a predetermined price to limit losses.

Take-Profit Orders: Set take-profit orders to automatically close a trade when it reaches a certain profit level.

Diversification: Spread your investments across different assets to mitigate risk.

5) Prepare Mentally and Emotionally

Emotional Control: Stay calm and avoid making impulsive decisions based on emotions.

Discipline: Stick to your trading plan and strategy, even when faced with market volatility.

6) Set Up Your Trading Environment

Reliable Trading Platform: Ensure you are using a reputable trading platform with the necessary tools and features.

Stable Internet Connection: Make sure you have a reliable and fast internet connection to avoid execution delays.

Comfortable Workspace: Set up a comfortable and distraction-free workspace to focus on your trading activities.

7) Monitor Economic and Market News

Economic Calendars: Keep track of upcoming economic events and announcements that may impact the markets.

News Feeds: Stay updated with the latest financial news and market developments.

8) Practice with a Demo Account

Simulated Trading: Use a demo account to practice your trading strategies and refine your skills without risking real money.

Backtesting: Test your trading strategies on historical data to evaluate their effectiveness.

9) Keep a Trading Journal

Record Keeping: Document all your trades, including the rationale, execution details, and outcomes.

Performance Review: Regularly review your journal to identify patterns, strengths, and areas for improvement.

"Trade What's Happening... Not What You Think Is Gonna Happen." — **Doug Gregory**

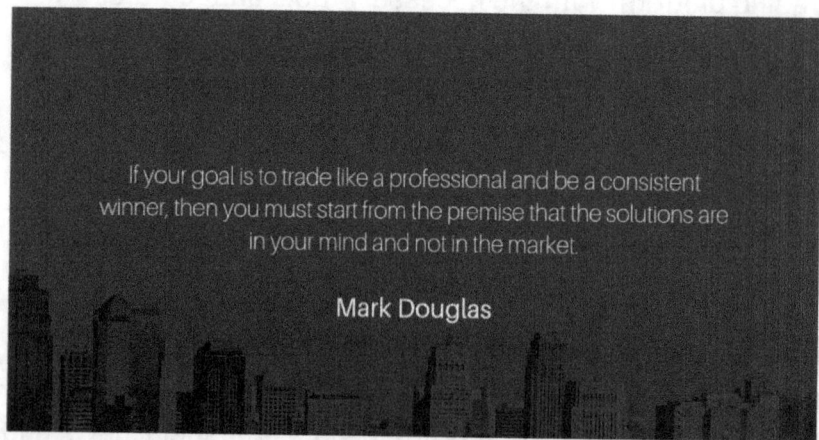

Strategy for Swing trading in Cash

1-Stock Selection
2-Trade Planning
3-Trading Psychology

1)Stock Selection-
(a)search for 52 week High stocks & All time high stocks
(b)Check Manually for each stock at Daily chart where the closing of the candle should be above previous high
(c)then check for Volume traded on same day
(d)If any stock follow above criteria……..then we can plan for trade.

2)Trade Planning-
(a)If the price move above previous day high mark, **BUY**
Ex-if previous day high is 98Rs ,If stock move above Rs100 BUY
(b)Holding period will be 1-8 days
(c)Stoploss will be previous day low or previous swing low
(d)Target will be ,Target1-1:1,Target2-1:2(Risk:Reward)

3)Trading Psychology-
(a)**Fear and Greed:** These are the two dominant emotions in trading. Fear can cause traders to exit positions too early, while greed may lead to holding on too long, hoping for more profit.
(b)**Journaling:** Keep a trading journal to record your thoughts, emotions, and rationale behind each trade. Reviewing this can reveal patterns in your trading behavior.

Real Estate: A Path to Sustainable Wealth

1. Introduction to Real Estate

Definition and Importance: Real estate involves property consisting of land and the buildings on it. It includes residential, commercial, industrial, and land investments. This segment provides substantial opportunities for wealth creation and diversification.

Historical Performance: Real estate has historically been a solid investment, often appreciating in value over time and providing rental income.

2. Types of Real Estate Investments

Residential Properties: Homes, apartments, and other living spaces. These can generate rental income and appreciate over time.

Commercial Properties: Office buildings, retail spaces, and warehouses. These are often leased to businesses and can provide stable income.

Industrial Properties: Factories, storage facilities, and distribution centers. These are crucial for logistics and manufacturing sectors.

Land: Raw land that can be developed or held for appreciation.

3. Benefits of Real Estate Investment

Appreciation: Over time, property values tend to rise, providing capital gains.

Income Generation: Rental properties can provide a steady stream of income.

Leverage: Using borrowed capital (mortgages) to increase the potential return on investment.

Tax Advantages: Various tax benefits, such as deductions on mortgage interest, property taxes, and depreciation.

4. Risks and Challenges
Market Volatility: Real estate markets can fluctuate based on economic conditions.
Liquidity Issues: Real estate is not as liquid as stocks or bonds, making it harder to quickly convert into cash.
Management and Maintenance: Properties require ongoing management and maintenance.
Regulatory Changes: Changes in zoning laws, property taxes, and rental regulations can impact investment returns.

5. Real Estate Investment Strategies
Buy and Hold: Purchasing properties to rent out and hold for long-term appreciation.
Flipping: Buying undervalued properties, renovating them, and selling them for a profit.
REITs (Real Estate Investment Trusts): Investing in companies that own, operate, or finance income-producing real estate. REITs provide a way to invest in real estate without owning physical property.

6. Real Estate and Wealth Building
Diversification: Real estate can diversify an investment portfolio, reducing overall risk.

Passive Income: Rental properties can provide a source of passive income, contributing to financial independence.

Inflation Hedge: Real estate often acts as a hedge against inflation, as property values and rents tend to rise with inflation.

7. Ethical and Sustainable Real Estate Investment

Sustainable Development: Investing in eco-friendly and sustainable properties.

Community Impact: Ensuring that real estate investments positively impact communities and provide affordable housing options.

Advantages and Disadvantages of Real Estate Investment

Advantages:

Appreciation

Benefit: Real estate properties typically increase in value over time. This appreciation can provide significant capital gains when the property is sold.

Example: A property purchased for $200,000 could appreciate to $300,000 over several years, yielding a $100,000 profit upon sale.

Income Generation

Benefit: Rental properties generate a steady stream of income. This can be a reliable source of passive income.

Example: Owning a rental property that generates $1,500 per month can provide $18,000 annually in rental income.

Leverage

Benefit: Investors can use borrowed funds (mortgages) to purchase real estate, amplifying their purchasing power and potential return on investment.

Example: With a $50,000 down payment, an investor can control a $250,000 property by taking out a mortgage.

Tax Benefits
Benefit: Real estate investors can take advantage of various tax deductions, such as mortgage interest, property taxes, and depreciation.
Example: Deductions for mortgage interest and depreciation can significantly reduce taxable income.

Hedge Against Inflation
Benefit: Real estate often appreciates in value and rental income increases with inflation, preserving purchasing power.
Example: As the cost of living rises, rental rates typically increase, providing a hedge against inflation.

Diversification
Benefit: Real estate adds diversification to an investment portfolio, reducing overall risk.
Example: Combining real estate with stocks and bonds can create a more balanced and resilient portfolio.

Disadvantages:
Market Volatility
Drawback: Real estate markets can be unpredictable and subject to economic conditions, leading to fluctuations in property values.
Example: A recession can lead to a decline in property values, impacting investment returns.

Liquidity Issues
Drawback: Real estate is not as easily converted to cash as other investments like stocks and bonds.
Example: Selling a property can take months, compared to the quick sale of stocks.

High Initial Costs

Drawback: Purchasing real estate requires significant upfront capital for down payments, closing costs, and initial repairs.

Example: Buying a property might require a 20% down payment, closing costs, and additional funds for any necessary renovations.

Management and Maintenance

Drawback: Real estate requires ongoing management and maintenance, which can be time-consuming and costly.

Example: Landlords must handle tenant issues, property repairs, and maintenance, which can be demanding.

Regulatory Changes

Drawback: Changes in laws and regulations, such as zoning laws, rent control, and property taxes, can impact profitability.

Example: New rent control laws might limit the ability to increase rental rates, affecting income.

Property Depreciation

Drawback: While land typically appreciates, buildings and structures can depreciate over time, requiring maintenance and renovations to retain value.

Example: An older property might need significant updates and repairs, which can be costly.

Financial Freedom

Financial freedom is the state of having sufficient personal wealth to live comfortably without the need to actively work for basic necessities. It means having enough income, investments, and savings to support your desired lifestyle and to achieve your financial goals without relying on regular employment.

Key aspects of financial freedom include:
Debt-Free Living: Having little to no debt, or at least managing debt in a way that doesn't hinder financial goals.
Emergency Fund: Having a savings cushion to cover unexpected expenses, which provides peace of mind.
Passive Income: Generating income from investments, real estate, or other sources that don't require active work.
Retirement Planning: Having enough savings and investments to support your lifestyle in retirement without financial stress.
Control Over Time: The ability to choose how to spend your time without being bound by financial obligations.
Wealth Preservation: Protecting your wealth through smart financial decisions, such as insurance, diversification, and estate planning.

Achieving financial freedom involves a combination of disciplined financial habits, strategic planning, and making informed decisions. Here are some key steps to guide you on this path:

1. Set Clear Financial Goals

Define What Freedom Means: Clearly outline your financial freedom goals, such as retirement age, lifestyle choices, and how much wealth you need.

Short-term and Long-term Goals: Break down your goals into short-term (e.g., paying off debt) and long-term (e.g., saving for retirement) to stay focused.

2. Create a Budget and Stick to It

Track Your Spending: Monitor your income and expenses to understand your financial habits.

Prioritize Savings: Allocate a portion of your income to savings and investments before spending on discretionary items.

Cut Unnecessary Expenses: Identify and reduce non-essential expenses to increase your savings rate.

3. Build an Emergency Fund

3-6 Months of Expenses: Save enough to cover 3-6 months of living expenses in case of unexpected events like job loss or medical emergencies.

Liquidity: Keep these funds in a liquid and easily accessible account, such as a high-yield savings account.

4. Pay Off Debt

Prioritize High-Interest Debt: Focus on paying off high-interest debts, such as credit cards, to reduce financial stress.

Debt Snowball/Avalanche Methods: Use these strategies to systematically eliminate debt and gain momentum.

5. Invest Wisely

Start Early: The earlier you start investing, the more time your money has to grow through compound interest.
Diversify: Spread your investments across different asset classes (stocks, bonds, real estate) to minimize risk.
Regular Contributions: Make consistent contributions to your investments, such as through retirement accounts (e.g., 401(k), IRA).

6. Generate Passive Income

Real Estate: Invest in rental properties or REITs (Real Estate Investment Trusts) to generate rental income.
Dividends: Invest in dividend-paying stocks or mutual funds to receive regular income.
Side Businesses: Create or invest in a business that can generate income with minimal effort.

7. Plan for Retirement

Contribute to Retirement Accounts: Maximize contributions to retirement accounts like 401(k), IRA, or similar plans to benefit from tax advantages.
Estimate Future Needs: Calculate how much you need to retire comfortably and create a plan to reach that goal.

Adjust for Inflation: Consider the impact of inflation on your retirement savings and adjust your strategy accordingly.

8. Protect Your Wealth

Insurance: Obtain adequate health, life, and disability insurance to protect against unforeseen events.
Estate Planning: Create a will and consider trusts to ensure your assets are distributed according to your wishes.

Diversify Risks: Avoid putting all your assets in one investment; spread your investments to reduce risk.

9. Continual Learning and Adaptation
Financial Education: Continuously educate yourself about personal finance, investing, and wealth management.
Adapt to Changes: Be flexible and adapt your financial strategies to changes in the economy, your personal situation, or new opportunities.

10. Stay Disciplined and Patient
Long-term Focus: Financial freedom is a marathon, not a sprint. Stay focused on your long-term goals and avoid short-term temptations.

The amount of money needed for financial freedom varies widely based on your lifestyle, location, retirement goals, and personal financial situation. However, there are some general guidelines and methods to estimate how much you need:

1. The 4% Rule

Basic Principle: The 4% rule suggests that you can withdraw 4% of your retirement savings each year, adjusted for inflation, and your money should last for at least 30 years.
How to Calculate: Multiply your annual living expenses by 25 to estimate how much you need. For example, if you need $50,000 per year, you would need $1.25 million ($50,000 x 25) in savings.

2. Estimate Based on Lifestyle

Annual Expenses: Calculate your current or expected annual living expenses during retirement. Include housing, food, healthcare, travel, hobbies, and other personal expenses.
Inflation Adjustment: Consider future inflation by increasing your estimated expenses by an annual inflation rate (e.g., 2-3% per year).
Emergency Fund: Include an emergency fund for unexpected expenses, such as medical emergencies or major repairs.

3. Net Worth Calculation

Assets vs. Liabilities: Determine your net worth by subtracting your total liabilities (debts) from your total assets (savings, investments, real estate, etc.).

Target Net Worth: Your target net worth for financial freedom should cover your annual expenses for the rest of your life without needing active income.

4. Passive Income Streams

Income Generation: Consider how much passive income (from investments, real estate, businesses, etc.) you can generate.

Supplementary Income: If your passive income can cover your living expenses, you may need less saved up for financial freedom.

5. Health and Longevity

Healthcare Costs: Account for potential healthcare costs, especially if you retire early and may not have employer-sponsored health insurance.

Longevity Risk: Consider the possibility of living longer than expected and needing more money for a longer retirement.

6. Personal Factors

Desired Retirement Age: The earlier you retire, the more you need, as your savings will need to last longer.

Lifestyle Choices: A modest lifestyle requires less, while a luxurious lifestyle requires significantly more.

Geographic Location: The cost of living varies greatly depending on where you live. Living in a high-cost city will require more savings than in a low-cost area.

"Being rich is having money; being wealthy is having time." —Margaret Bonnano.

Example Calculations:
Modest Lifestyle:
Annual Expenses: Rs40,000
Required Savings: Rs40,000 x 25 = Rs1 million

Comfortable Lifestyle:
Annual Expenses: Rs70,000
Required Savings: Rs70,000 x 25 = Rs1.75 million

Luxurious Lifestyle:
Annual Expenses: Rs150,000
Required Savings: Rs150,000 x 25 = Rs3.75 million

The ideal age to achieve financial retirement varies depending on individual goals, financial habits, lifestyle choices, and the effectiveness of your financial planning. However, common retirement ages and considerations include:

1. Traditional Retirement Age (65-67)
Social Security Benefits: In many countries, this is the age when full Social Security or pension benefits become available.
Health Considerations: At this age, many people may slow down physically and desire to retire from work.

2. Early Retirement (40-55)
FIRE Movement (Financial Independence, Retire Early): Some people aim to retire in their 40s or 50s by saving aggressively, investing wisely, and living frugally.
Higher Savings Rate: Requires a high savings rate (50-70% of income) and substantial investments to sustain a long retirement.

3. Very Early Retirement (30-40)
Extreme Financial Planning: Requires extreme financial discipline, high income, or entrepreneurial success, combined with a minimalist lifestyle.

Significant Passive Income: Building substantial passive income streams (real estate, dividends, business) is crucial to sustain a very long retirement.

4. Late Retirement (70+)

Continued Work: Some people choose or need to work longer due to financial necessity or personal satisfaction.
Increased Savings: Continued employment allows for increased savings and potentially higher retirement benefits.

Key Considerations for Deciding Your Retirement Age:

Financial Preparedness: How much you've saved and invested to support your desired lifestyle.
Health and Longevity: Your health and family history can impact how long you want or need to work.
Lifestyle Choices: The lifestyle you envision during retirement (travel, hobbies, etc.) and the associated costs.
Debt Levels: Having little to no debt can allow for earlier retirement.

Income Streams: Passive income streams or part-time work can supplement retirement savings, allowing for earlier retirement.

Inflation and Economic Factors: Consider inflation, market conditions, and economic stability in your retirement planning.

Becoming financially free at an early age requires discipline, strategic planning, and sometimes a willingness to make sacrifices. Here are some of the best ways to achieve financial freedom early in life:
1. Start Early

Invest in Education: Gain financial literacy by learning about budgeting, investing, and money management. The earlier you start, the more time you have to compound your wealth.
Begin Investing Young: Start investing as soon as possible to take full advantage of compound interest. Even small investments can grow significantly over time.

2. Live Below Your Means
Frugality: Adopt a lifestyle that prioritizes saving and investing over spending. Avoid lifestyle inflation as your income increases.

Minimalism: Focus on needs rather than wants, reducing unnecessary expenses and freeing up more money for savings and investments.

"Anyone who stops learning is old, whether at twenty or eighty. Anyone who keeps learning stays young. The greatest thing in life is to keep your mind young." – Henry Ford

3. Aggressively Save and Invest
High Savings Rate: Aim to save and invest 50% or more of your income. This requires living on a tight budget but significantly accelerates wealth accumulation.
Automatic Investments: Set up automatic transfers to your investment accounts to ensure you consistently invest a portion of your income.

4. Maximize Income
Career Advancement: Focus on acquiring skills and education that can increase your earning potential. Negotiate for higher salaries and seek promotions.

Side Hustles: Start side businesses or freelancing gigs to generate additional income streams. Use this extra income exclusively for investments.

Passive Income: Invest in assets that generate passive income, such as dividend stocks, rental properties, or online businesses.

5. Debt Management

Avoid High-Interest Debt: Stay clear of credit card debt and other high-interest loans that can hinder your financial progress.

Debt Payoff Strategies: If you have debt, use strategies like the debt snowball or avalanche method to pay it off quickly, freeing up more income for savings and investments.

6. Invest Wisely

Diversify Investments: Spread your investments across different asset classes (stocks, bonds, real estate) to reduce risk and increase potential returns.

Real Estate Investing: Consider investing in rental properties, which can generate passive income and appreciate in value over time.

Stock Market: Invest in index funds, ETFs, or individual stocks for long-term growth. Focus on low-cost, diversified funds that match your risk tolerance.

7. Embrace the FIRE Movement

Financial Independence, Retire Early (FIRE): This approach involves extreme saving and investing to achieve financial independence in your 30s or 40s.

Lean FIRE: Achieving financial freedom with a frugal lifestyle, requiring less savings.

Fat FIRE: Achieving financial freedom with a more comfortable lifestyle, requiring higher savings.

8. Control Lifestyle Inflation
Maintain a Consistent Lifestyle: As your income grows, resist the temptation to increase your spending proportionally.
Invest Raises and Bonuses: Instead of spending income increases, invest them to accelerate your journey to financial freedom.

9. Build Multiple Income Streams
Diversify Income Sources: Having multiple streams of income (e.g., job, investments, business) reduces risk and accelerates wealth building.
Entrepreneurship: Starting your own business can be a powerful way to increase income, though it comes with risks and requires careful planning.

10. Stay Disciplined and Patient
Long-Term Focus: Keep your eyes on the long-term goal of financial freedom. Avoid get-rich-quick schemes and stay disciplined in your saving and investing habits.
Regular Reviews: Regularly review your financial plan, making adjustments as needed to stay on track.

11. Leverage Tax-Advantaged Accounts
Retirement Accounts: Maximize contributions to tax-advantaged retirement accounts like a 401(k), IRA, or Roth IRA to benefit from tax savings and compound growth.
Health Savings Account (HSA): Use an HSA for tax-free medical savings, which can also grow as an investment if not used for current medical expenses.

12. Protect Your Wealth

Insurance: Ensure you have appropriate insurance coverage (health, life, disability) to protect against unforeseen events.
Emergency Fund: Maintain an emergency fund to cover unexpected expenses without derailing your financial plan.

B. Mastering the Art of Budgeting and Financial Planning

Mastering the art of budgeting and financial planning involves understanding and applying key principles to manage your money effectively.

(A) Set Clear Goals: Define your short-term and long-term financial goals, such as saving for a vacation, buying a house, or retiring comfortably.

(B) Track Your Income and Expenses: Keep track of how much money you earn and where you spend it. Use tools like spreadsheets or budgeting apps to categorize your expenses.

(C)Create a Budget: Based on your income and expenses, create a budget that allocates money for essentials like housing, food, transportation, and savings. Be realistic and flexible.

(D)Prioritize Saving: Make saving a priority by setting aside a portion of your income for emergencies, investments, and future goals. Aim to save at least 10-20% of your income.

(E)Minimize Debt: Try to minimize high-interest debt like credit cards. Pay off debts systematically, starting with the ones with the highest interest rates.

(F)Invest Wisely: Learn about different investment options such as stocks, bonds, mutual funds, and real estate. Consider your risk tolerance and investment goals before making decisions.

(G)Review and Adjust: Regularly review your budget and financial goals. Make adjustments as needed to stay on track and achieve your objectives.

(H)Seek Professional Advice: If needed, consult with financial advisors or planners to get personalized guidance on investments, taxes, and retirement planning.

C. Investing with Wisdom and Ethics: Building Sustainable Wealth

(A)Understanding Your Values: Before investing, think about what matters most to you. Are you passionate about environmental sustainability, social justice, or ethical business practices? Knowing your values helps guide your investment choices.

(B)Researching Companies: Look into the companies you're considering investing in. Are they transparent about their practices, such as how they treat employees, their environmental impact, and their governance structure? Seek out companies that align with your values and have a track record of ethical behavior.

(C)Diversification: Spread your investments across different asset classes, industries, and geographic regions. Diversification helps reduce risk by not putting all your eggs in one basket. It's like having a variety of crops in a farm to ensure a bad season for one doesn't ruin everything.

(D)Long-Term Perspective: Invest with a long-term mindset. Sustainable wealth isn't built overnight but through consistent, thoughtful investing over time. Avoid getting swayed by short-term market fluctuations or trends.

(E)Risk Management: Be aware of the risks associated with each investment. Understand the potential for loss and have strategies in place to mitigate risks, such as setting stop-loss orders or having a diversified portfolio.

(F)Impact Investing: Consider impact investing, where you intentionally invest in companies or funds that have a positive impact on society or the environment. This could include renewable energy projects, affordable housing initiatives, or companies promoting diversity and inclusion.

(G)Review and Adjust: Regularly review your investments and financial goals. Adjust your portfolio as needed to stay aligned with your values, risk tolerance, and long-term objectives.

D. Giving Back: Enriching Lives through Charity and Service

(A) Identifying Causes: Start by identifying causes or issues that resonate with you. It could be supporting education, healthcare, environmental conservation, poverty alleviation, or any other area where you want to make a difference.

(B) Researching Organizations: Once you know your cause, research reputable organizations that work in that field. Look for transparency, efficiency in using donations, and tangible impact on communities or individuals.

(C) Volunteering: Volunteering your time and skills is a powerful way to give back. Whether it's tutoring children, assisting in a soup kitchen, or participating in environmental cleanups, your contribution can directly benefit those in need.

(D) Donating Money: Financial contributions are also valuable. You can donate to nonprofits, charities, or crowdfunding campaigns that align with your values and have a proven track record of effective use of funds.

(E) Fundraising: Organize fundraising events or campaigns to raise money for a cause. This could involve hosting charity dinners, running marathons for a cause, or creating online fundraising campaigns through social media platforms.

(F) Corporate Social Responsibility (CSR): If you're part of a business or organization, consider incorporating CSR initiatives. This could include donating a percentage of profits to charity, implementing eco-friendly practices, or providing employee volunteering opportunities.

(G)Impact Measurement: Evaluate the impact of your charitable efforts. Monitor how your donations or volunteer work are making a difference and adjust your strategies if needed to maximize positive outcomes.

(H)Educating Others: Spread awareness about the importance of giving back. Encourage others to join you in charitable activities, whether it's friends, family, colleagues, or your community.

E.Seeking Guidance: Navigating Wealth Management with Expertise

(A)Financial Goals: Start by defining your financial goals. Do you want to save for retirement, buy a home, start a business, or fund your children's education? Having clear goals helps guide your wealth management strategy.

(B)Budgeting: Create a budget to track your income and expenses. Know how much you're earning, how much you're spending, and where your money is going. This helps you identify areas where you can save and invest more effectively.

(C)Saving and Investing: Save a portion of your income regularly and invest it wisely. Understand different investment options such as stocks, bonds, mutual funds, real estate, and retirement accounts. Diversify your investments to manage risk.

(D)Risk Assessment: Assess your risk tolerance. Are you comfortable with higher-risk investments that offer potentially higher returns, or do you prefer lower-risk options with more stability? Your risk tolerance influences your investment decisions.

(E)Tax Planning: Consider tax implications in your wealth management strategy. Explore tax-efficient investment vehicles and strategies to minimize tax liabilities and maximize returns.

(F)Estate Planning: Plan for the future by creating an estate plan. This includes writing a will, setting up trusts, designating beneficiaries, and ensuring your assets are distributed according to your wishes.

(G)Insurance: Protect your wealth and assets with insurance coverage. This may include health insurance, life insurance, property insurance, and liability insurance. Review your insurance needs regularly.

(H)Professional Advice: Consider consulting with financial advisors, accountants, and estate planners. They can provide expert guidance tailored to your specific financial situation and goals.

(I)Continuous Learning: Stay informed about financial markets, economic trends, and investment opportunities. Continuous learning helps you make informed decisions and adapt your wealth management strategy as needed.

(J)Review and Adjust: Regularly review your financial plan and investment portfolio. Adjust your strategy based on changes in your goals, risk tolerance, market conditions, and life circumstances

"You can have excuses or you can have success; you can't have both." — Jen Sincero

VII. Conclusion
A. Recapitulating the Gita's Wisdom on Wealth Mastery

"The Bhagavad Gita offers timeless insights into mastering wealth that go beyond mere financial abundance. It teaches us that true wealth encompasses material prosperity, spiritual fulfillment, and emotional well-being. By following the path of Karma Yoga, which emphasizes selfless action and the service of others, we can achieve not only financial success but also inner peace and happiness.

Budgeting and financial planning are essential tools on this journey, helping us manage resources wisely and align our actions with our values. Investing with wisdom and ethics ensures that our wealth grows sustainably and contributes positively to society. Moreover, enriching lives through charity and service allows us to share our abundance and make a meaningful difference in the world.

Ultimately, mastering wealth is not just about accumulating riches but about living a balanced and fulfilling life. The Gita's wisdom reminds us that wealth, when managed with expertise and integrity, can be a powerful means to create a better future for ourselves and others."

B. Integrating Spiritual Principles into Financial Success

"As we conclude our exploration of financial success, it's crucial to recognize the profound impact of integrating spiritual principles into our approach. Beyond the traditional metrics of wealth, true success encompasses inner fulfillment, harmony, and a sense of purpose.

By aligning our financial goals with spiritual values such as integrity, compassion, and mindfulness, we not only achieve material prosperity but also cultivate a deeper sense of well-being. This integration allows us to make decisions that are not only profitable but also ethical and sustainable, benefiting not just ourselves but also our communities and the planet.

Practices like gratitude, generosity, and conscious consumption play a pivotal role in this journey. They remind us to appreciate what we have, share our blessings with others, and make mindful choices that honor our interconnectedness with all beings.

Ultimately, spiritual principles infuse our pursuit of financial success with meaning and significance. They guide us to create wealth not just for personal gain but for the greater good, fostering a more prosperous and harmonious world for generations to come."

C. Embracing Holistic Prosperity: The Journey Ahead

"As we come to the end of our discussion on holistic prosperity, it's clear that true wealth extends far beyond financial riches. It encompasses our physical well-being, mental clarity, emotional balance, and spiritual fulfillment.

The journey ahead is one of integration and balance. It involves nurturing our health through exercise, nutrition, and self-care practices that support our overall well-being. It also requires cultivating a positive mindset, resilience, and inner peace, which are invaluable assets in navigating life's challenges.

Embracing holistic prosperity means honoring our relationships and connections with others, fostering meaningful connections, and prioritizing love, compassion, and empathy. It's about finding purpose and alignment with our values, living authentically, and contributing positively to the world around us.

As we embark on this journey, let us remember that true prosperity is a state of wholeness, where every aspect of our being is nurtured and thriving. It's not just about what we accumulate, but how we live, grow, and impact the lives of others. May our pursuit of holistic prosperity bring us joy, fulfillment, and a deep sense of fulfillment."

www.ingramcontent.com/pod-product-compliance
Lightning Source LLC
Chambersburg PA
CBHW052201220526
45471CB00004B/1760